#Follow Me
#Artist Developer

GeeGee Miller

#Follow Me

#Artist Developer

Disclaimer

This book is for informational and educational purposes only and does not constitute legal, tax, or financial advice. While every effort has been made to ensure the accuracy of the information contained herein, the author and publisher make no warranties, express or implied, and assume no responsibility for errors or omissions. Readers are encouraged to consult qualified professionals regarding specific circumstances. Any references to laws, regulations, payment rates, platform policies, or royalty figures may change over time.

Trademarks

All trademarks, service marks, product names, and company names mentioned in this book are the property of their respective owners. Their use in this book does not imply endorsement,

Cataloging and Identifiers

ISBN (Paperback): 979-8-9935513-0-2

Publisher Information

Published by: Clock Publisher

Credits

Cover Design: GeeGee Miller
Formatting: Clock Publisher
Editor: Clock Publisher

Printing Details

First Edition: 2026
Printed in the United States of America

Welcome! I'm **#ArtistDeveloper @GeeGee Miller**, your Artist Music Business Developer, and I'm truly excited to begin this journey with you. If you've already seen results from my first book, *HOW TO SIGN YOURSELF*, prepare to move forward with confidence. This edition has been fully enhanced, thoroughly refreshed, and refined into one of the most focused and practical guides to music business independence available today. All I ask from you is committed time and a distraction-free environment. In return, you'll build a rock-solid foundation for your career.

BOOK OUTLINE

Mastering Your Music Career: Registration, Independence, and Business Savvy

Course Overview

This course is created for beginner musicians and songwriters who are ready to take ownership of their music careers. By learning why music registration matters, how to remain independent, and how the business side of the industry truly works, you will gain the confidence and clarity needed to move forward with purpose and control.

1: Understanding Music Registration

1.1 The Importance of Music Registration

- A clear explanation of music registration and why it matters

- The financial and legal risks of leaving works unregistered

- Essential terms: Copyright, PROs, MLC, ISRC

1.2 How to Register Your Music

- A step-by-step walkthrough of registering with a Performance Rights Organization (PRO)

- Understanding The MLC and how it collects mechanical royalties

- How to properly obtain, assign, and manage ISRC codes

1.3 Common Registration Mistakes

- How to recognize and avoid common registration errors

- Why accurate metadata is critical to royalty collection

- Real-world examples of artists losing income due to incorrect registrations

1.4 Action Steps

- A practical checklist for registering your music correctly

- Trusted tools and resources for continued learning

2. Staying Independent in the Music Industry

2.1 The Value of Independence

- What independence truly means in today's music industry

- The advantages of staying independent versus signing with a label

2.2 Building Your Brand as an Independent Artist

- Techniques for shaping a strong and authentic artistic identity

- Why social media and online presence matter more than ever

- Networking strategies tailored for independent musicians

2.3 Monetizing Your Music Independently

- An overview of income sources such as streaming, licensing, and merchandise

- How to effectively use platforms like Bandcamp, Patreon, and similar services

- The role digital distribution plays in revenue growth

2.4 Action Steps

- Create a personalized artist branding plan

- Develop a clear and realistic monetization strategy

3. Understanding the Music Business

3.1 The Basics of the Music Business

- A breakdown of the modern music industry ecosystem

- Key industry roles including managers, agents, publishers, and labels

- A practical introduction to contracts and agreements

3.2 Financial Literacy for Musicians

- Core budgeting and money-management principles

- How royalties are generated and calculated

- Basic tax considerations for independent artists

3.3 Navigating the Legal Landscape

- An introduction to copyright law and why it matters

- Ways to safeguard your music and intellectual property

- Resources for professional legal guidance

3.4 Action Steps

- Build a simple working budget for your music career

- Learn foundational contract and legal terminology

4. Taking Action and Moving Forward

4.1 Creating Your Action Plan

- Combining everything you've learned into a single, workable plan

- Setting achievable short-term and long-term career goals

4.2 Building a Support Network

- Identifying mentors, collaborators, and peers

- Why community and collaboration matter

- How to engage with local and online music scenes

4.3 Staying Motivated and Inspired

- Strategies to maintain creativity and momentum

- Building resilience through challenges

- Recognizing and celebrating progress

4.4 Final Thoughts and Next Steps

- A recap of the most important takeaways

- Encouragement to take immediate, intentional action

- Resources for continued education and growth

This course outline provides a complete framework for beginners who want to understand music registration, independence, and the business realities of the industry. Each section builds on the last, ensuring you walk away with actionable knowledge and a clear direction for your music business journey.

Q. Are you an artist or producer ready to take control of your career and increase your earning potential?

Ans. As your Artist Music Business Developer, I focus on breaking down the Royalty Collection System in a way that makes sense. Many artists are registered with BMI, ASCAP, SoundExchange, and distributors, yet still don't know how to fully use them to their advantage.

Q. Ready to create your own music empire?

Ans. I'll walk you through building your personal "Label" formula, whether your goal is to benefit entirely on your own or grow with a team.

In this book, you'll learn how to structure your business to maximize royalties and income streams so everyone involved is positioned for success. From understanding the **Royalty Collection System** to claiming all 10–16 revenue streams tied to a single song, this guide is designed to help you take control and build a sustainable, profitable career.

You'll learn how to properly establish yourself as an independent artist while retaining 100% ownership of your work. Discover how one song can generate 10–16 income streams and how to align them for maximum impact. From songwriter to publisher, I'll guide you through claiming every role and revenue source available to you.

Unlock 10–16 revenue streams from a single song. I help artists and producers navigate the music industry through my Artist Development Process, covering royalty collection, ownership, self-marketing, and more. Learn how to wear every hat, songwriter, composer, publisher, distributor, and truly **Sign Yourself** to a lifetime of earnings.

I empower artists, producers, and managers to monetize their music independently. **My Artist Development Process** simplifies royalty collection, ownership, and strategic self-marketing so you can understand your income streams and retain full ownership, without relying on a label. Sign yourself and get paid for life.

This book is designed to help you uncover how to get paid for your music. As your **Artist Music Business Developer**, I guide you through the **Royalty Collection System,** so you know exactly how and when you earn every time someone presses play. Learn how to build your independent empire and keep 100% ownership of your music. Let's maximize your revenue streams.

<u>Alright. Buckle up. Let's begin your Artist Music Business Development!</u>

Table of Contents

Chapter 1: Understanding the Royalty Collection System

Objectives:

1. Understand the importance of the Royalty Collection System

2. Learn WHY you need an understanding of the Royalty Collection System

3. Learn THE HOW of the Royalty Collection System

Understanding the music royalty collection system is arguably the **most essential business skill** a musician or songwriter can develop. It is the operational structure that transforms creative output into **long-term, sustainable income.**

Objective 1.1: Understand the Importance of the Royalty Collection System

The music industry operates through a layered network of intellectual property rights, licenses, and collection agencies designed to compensate creators. Grasping how this system functions means recognizing the **multiple, separate revenue streams** that can originate from a single song.

Key Concept	Description
Two Core Copyrights	Every song contains **two distinct copyrights**, and each copyright produces its own category of income. These copyrights exist independently of one another and must be managed separately.

Every song has **two separate copyrights**, which generate two separate sets of royalties:

- **The Composition** (lyrics, melody, chords, arrangement), owned by the **Songwriter**

Together, these two copyrights generate **four primary royalty streams: Performance, Mechanical, Master Recording**, and **Synchronization**. Each stream follows its own collection pathway and requires separate registration.

Key Concept	Description
Maximizing Earnings	Registering only with a distributor limits what you collect. Without full registration, significant revenue tied to the composition side of the song remains unpaid to you.

If you register only with a digital distributor, you will collect **Master Recording** royalties and limited **Streaming Performance** income. You will not receive the additional, independent revenue streams connected to the *Composition*, such as **mechanical royalties, terrestrial radio performance income**, and **international royalties.**

Objective 1.2: Learn WHY You Need Understanding of the Royalty Collection System

Reason	Impact on Your Career
Financial Security	Proper registration ensures you collect **100% of the income you are entitled to.** Failure to affiliate with the correct organizations (PROs, The MLC, SoundExchange) on the composition side can result in up to half of your earnings being lost to the industry's "black box" of unclaimed royalties.
Metadata Accuracy	You learn *which* identifiers matter (ISRC, ISWC, Split Sheets) and *where* each must be submitted. Incorrect or missing data is the leading cause of lost royalty payments.
Negotiation Power	You gain the ability to negotiate fair agreements with collaborators, producers, publishers, and labels because you understand the real value of the rights being administered. Knowledge prevents exploitation.
Global Collection	You recognize that U.S. PROs (ASCAP/BMI) do not collect every royalty worldwide, and that a **Publishing Administrator** (such as Songtrust or a publisher/administrator) may be necessary for international performance and mechanical royalties.

Avoiding Disputes	Maintaining a written **Split Sheet** and ensuring all collaborators properly register their ownership prevents legal conflicts and future ownership challenges.

Objective 1.3: Learn THE HOW of the Royalty Collection System

The most practical way to understand this system is to break it down into the **four core royalty categories** and then take the required action to register for each one.

The Four Pillars of Royalties

Royalty Type	Generated When...	Collected By	Paid To
Master Recording	Your recording is streamed, downloaded, or sold. Revenue is tied to ownership of the *sound recording*.	**Your Distributor** (DistroKid, TuneCore, CD Baby)	Artist / Label
Performance	The *composition* is performed publicly (radio, TV, background music, live venues, streaming services).	**PROs** (ASCAP, BMI, SESAC)	**Songwriter / Publisher**
Mechanical	The *composition* is reproduced through	**The MLC** (U.S. streaming)	**Songwriter / Publisher**

	physical sales, digital downloads, or streaming (each stream counts as a reproduction).		
Digital Performance	Your *sound recording* is played on **non-interactive** digital radio platforms (Pandora, SiriusXM, webcasters).	**SoundExchange**	**Artist / Session Musicians / Label**

Action Plan: Essential Registrations

To collect **100% of your royalties**, you must register with the following entities if you are both the songwriter and the recording artist:

1. **Distributor**

   Upload your music and metadata (artist name, ISRC) to a distributor to collect **Master Recording royalties**.

2. **Performing Rights Organization (PRO)**

   Join **one** PRO (such as **ASCAP** or **BMI**) as a **Writer** and establish your own **Publisher** entity to collect both the writer's and publisher's shares of **Performance royalties**.

3. **The Mechanical Licensing Collective (MLC)**

   Register your songs and ownership splits (ISWC, publisher details) to collect **U.S. mechanical royalties** from streaming services.

4. **SoundExchange**

   Register as both a **Performer** and **Rights Owner** to receive **Digital Performance royalties** from non-interactive streaming.

5. **Publishing Administrator (Optional but Recommended)**

   Consider a publishing administrator (Songtrust, Sentric, or distributor publishing arms) to manage **international mechanical and performance royalties**.

THE PRINCIPLE IS SIMPLE:

If you created the song, you have **two income sources**. You must register with the organizations responsible for both the **Composition** (PRO, MLC) and the **Sound Recording** (Distributor, SoundExchange).

Chapter 2: Finding Listeners and the Self-Booking Process

Objectives:

1. Understand the importance of Finding Listeners and the Self-Booking Process

2. Learn WHY these systems are necessary

3. Learn HOW to develop Finding Listeners and the Self-Booking Process

These objectives focus on the **career-building mechanics** of an independent musician, specifically the relationship between **audience growth** and **live performance opportunities**.

Objective 2.1: Understand the Importance of Finding Listeners and the Self-Booking Process

Component	Importance
Finding Listeners (Audience Building)	The foundation of a sustainable music career. Fans purchase merchandise, tickets, and provide direct financial support through platforms like Patreon or Bandcamp,

	which often generate the most reliable income for independent artists.
Algorithmic Momentum	Listener behaviors such as full streams, saves, shares, and playlist adds signal engagement to streaming algorithms (Spotify, Apple Music), increasing recommendations through features like Discover Weekly and Release Radar.
Live Performance Demand	Venues and promoters prioritize artists who can **draw an audience**. The size and engagement of your listener base directly affect your booking value.

The Self-Booking Process (DIY Gigs and Tours) is the **engine of growth and independence** for self-managed artists.

Benefit	Explanation
Artistic Control & Experience	You choose venues, dates, and collaborators, allowing alignment with your creative direction while learning the business firsthand.
Building a Network	Direct interaction with venue owners, promoters, and other artists builds relationships essential for future opportunities.
Proof of Concept	Successfully booking and promoting shows demonstrates professionalism, reliability, and audience demand to agents, managers, and labels.

Objective 2.2: Learn WHY You Need Finding Listeners and the Self-Booking Process

These two systems are essential because they are the **only sustainable path** for independent artists to grow without major label backing or large upfront investment.

- **They Validate Each Other**
    - **Finding Listeners** provides the data you use to pitch venues.
    - **Self-Booking** converts casual listeners into long-term fans, accelerating audience growth.
- **It Keeps You in Control**
  You own your data, your relationships, and your timeline. Relying entirely on third parties such as social platforms or booking agents leaves your career vulnerable to decisions outside your control.

Objective 2.3: Learn HOW to Build Finding Listeners and the Self-Booking Process

HOW to Get Your Finding Listeners (Data-Driven System)

Strategy	Action Items

Optimize Digital Presence	Maintain professional recordings, photos, and a clearly defined artist brand and story.
Analytics	Use Spotify for Artists and social insights to understand **who**, **where**, and **how** your audience listens. This data becomes your leverage.
Platform Strategy	Pitch releases through Spotify for Artists and connect with independent playlist curators aligned with your sound.
Social Engagement	Create short-form video content (TikTok, Reels) that showcases personality and story. Actively engage through comments and messages.
Direct Connection	Build and maintain an email list using incentives like exclusive content or downloads.
Call-to-Action	Teach fans how to support you: full streams, saves, follows, merchandise purchases.

HOW to Get Your Self-Booking Process

Step	Action Items
Preparation	Create a professional **Electronic Press Kit (EPK)** including bio, music links, live footage, social metrics, and press. Research venues that match your genre and draw size.
Outreach	Personalize every pitch. Reference recent events at the venue and clearly explain why your music fits their audience.
Professional Pitching	Use concise subject lines and emails. Include links to your EPK and analytics demonstrating local draw.

Execution	Promote relentlessly using your listener system. Ticket sales are your responsibility.
Follow-Up	Send a thank-you message after each show with a photo and express interest in future bookings.

Chapter 3: Navigating the Performance Rights Organization Landscape

Performance Rights Organizations

Objectives:

1. Understand the importance of Performance Rights Organizations

2. Learn WHY you need the Performance Rights Organization process collection system

3. Learn HOW to get your music registered with Performance Rights Organizations

This set of objectives centers on **Performance Rights Organizations (PROs)**, which are a foundational financial and legal pillar of a songwriter's career, especially for independent musicians.

Below is a structured breakdown addressing each objective.

Objective 3.1: Understand the Importance of Performance Rights Organizations

A **Performance Rights Organization (PRO)** is an entity that collects **public performance royalties** on behalf of songwriters, composers, and music publishers. PROs act as an essential financial and legal intermediary within the music industry ecosystem.

Why PROs Matter

Ensures Compensation for Public Use

PROs make sure you are paid whenever your original music is publicly performed. Public performance includes:

- **Radio:** AM/FM, satellite radio, and internet radio
- **Television:** Films, TV shows, commercials, and background music in programming
- **Live Venues:** Clubs, bars, concert halls, festivals
- **Commercial Public Spaces:** Restaurants, retail stores, gyms, hotels
- **Digital Streaming Services:** Spotify, Apple Music, Pandora, when used in non-interactive or public contexts such as internet radio channels

Simplifies Licensing for Music Users

Instead of a business owner needing to locate and pay thousands of individual songwriters, venues purchase a single annual

blanket license from a PRO. This license legally covers the public performance of millions of songs within that PRO's catalog.

Tracks Music Usage Worldwide

PROs rely on advanced tracking systems such as cue sheets, digital monitoring tools, and detailed usage reports. Through reciprocal agreements with international societies, they monitor performances globally and ensure royalties are collected across borders.

Objective 3.2: Learn WHY You Need the Performance Rights Organization Collection System

You need this system to collect money you are legally entitled to as the copyright holder of the **composition**. If your music is performed publicly and you are not registered, those royalties are either held indefinitely or distributed to other registered members. You do not receive them.

To Collect Your Songwriter Share

This share is paid directly to the individual who wrote the lyrics and/or composed the music.

To Collect Your Publisher Share

Even if you are an independent artist without a traditional publishing deal, you must register a publishing entity with your PRO.

If you do not, you collect only the songwriter portion and lose **50% of your earned performance royalties**.

To Receive Payment for Live Performances

U.S. PROs such as ASCAP and BMI offer programs like **ASCAP OnStage** and **BMI Live**. These systems allow you to submit setlists of original music performed at licensed venues and receive direct payments for those performances.

To Establish Official Copyright Metadata

Registering a song with a PRO creates essential identifiers such as the **ISWC (International Standard Musical Work Code)**. This metadata is used across the industry to ensure your name and ownership are accurately linked to your work.

Objective 3.3: Learn HOW to Get Your Music Registered with Performance Rights Organizations

The registration process involves two affiliations and song registration.

Step 1: Choose and Join a PRO

In the United States, your primary options include:

- **ASCAP (American Society of Composers, Authors and Publishers):** Non-profit

- **BMI (Broadcast Music, Inc.):** Non-profit

- **SESAC:** For-profit and invitation-only

Action Steps

Choose One PRO

You may only affiliate as a writer with **one** PRO at a time. Compare fees, payout schedules, and member benefits such as workshops and discounts.

Affiliate as a Writer

Apply through the PRO's website to become a songwriter member. You will receive a unique identifier known as an **IPI or CAE number**.

Affiliate as a Publisher

If you own your publishing rights, create a separate publishing entity and affiliate it with the same PRO. This usually requires a one-time fee ranging from $50 to $250.

Step 2: Register Your Musical Works

Once both accounts are active, register each song.

Action Steps

1. Log in to your PRO member portal

2. Select "Works Registration" or "Register a Song"

3. Enter required information:

   - **Song Title**

- **Co-Writer Information:** Names, PRO affiliations, IPI numbers

- **Song Splits:** Writer and publisher percentages must each total 100%

- **Performing Artist and Recording Info:** Artist name and ISRC from your distributor

Step 3: Report Live Performances

Action Steps

1. Log into your PRO's live performance system

2. Submit the performance date, venue, and setlist of original songs

NOTE: Many independent artists simplify this entire process by using a **publishing administrator** such as Songtrust or a distributor-based publishing service, which handles global registration and collection for a fee or royalty percentage.

Chapter 4: SoundExchange

Objectives:

1. Understand the importance of SoundExchange

2. Learn WHY you need SoundExchange

3. Learn HOW to register your music with SoundExchange

This chapter focuses on **SoundExchange**, an organization frequently confused with PROs but responsible for an entirely different and critical royalty stream.

Key Difference: PROs vs. SoundExchange

Organization	Royalties Collected	Copyright Type	Who Gets Paid	Source of Performance
PROs (ASCAP, BMI, SESAC)	Performance royalties	Composition (lyrics and melody)	Songwriter and Publisher	Radio, live venues, TV, non-interactive streaming

SoundExchange	Digital performance royalties	Sound Recording (Master)	Featured Artist and Sound Recording Copyright Owner	Non-interactive digital streaming

Objective 4.1: Understand the Importance of SoundExchange

SoundExchange is the **only organization in the United States** authorized by Congress to collect and distribute **digital performance royalties for sound recordings.**

The Only Way to Get Paid for Digital Radio Plays

If your music plays on non-interactive platforms such as SiriusXM, Pandora (free tier), or webcasters, SoundExchange is the sole collection pathway.

Direct Payment to Artists

Featured artists receive 45% directly, and non-featured performers receive 5%, regardless of recoupment status with a label.

Global Collection

Through reciprocal agreements, SoundExchange collects international neighboring rights royalties worldwide.

Objective 4.2: Learn WHY You Need SoundExchange

SoundExchange pays royalties tied to the **sound recording**, not the composition.

Royalty Breakdown

- **50%** to the Sound Recording Copyright Owner

- **45%** to the Featured Artist

- **5%** to Non-Featured Performers

If You Do Not Register

- Unclaimed royalties are held for approximately **three years**

- After that, funds may be redistributed

- You permanently lose that income

SoundExchange also serves as your gateway to international neighboring rights, which are otherwise inaccessible to individuals.

Objective 4.3: Learn HOW to Register Your Music with SoundExchange

Registration is **free** and completed once.

Step 1: Register Your Account

- Visit the official SoundExchange website

- Register as a **Performer**, **SRCO**, or both

- Provide tax and banking information

- Sign the Membership and Mandate Agreement for global collection

Step 2: Claim Your Recordings

- Log into SoundExchange Direct

- Search using **ISRC codes**

- Claim your recordings and specify ownership roles

Required Information

- Legal name or company name

- Tax ID

- ISRCs

- Featured artist names

- Label or copyright owner name

Chapter 5: Copyright

Objectives:

1. Understand the importance of copyright registration

2. Learn WHY you need copyright protection

3. Learn HOW to register your lyrics and beats

Copyright protects two related works: the **Musical Work** and the **Sound Recording**. Formal registration provides the strongest legal protection.

Objective 5.1: Understand the Importance of Copyright Registration

In the United States, registration with the **U.S. Copyright Office** forms the legal foundation of music ownership.

Public Record of Ownership

Registration establishes a public, legally recognized claim and serves as **prima facie evidence** in court.

Facilitates Licensing

Registration makes ownership transparent and enables licensing opportunities. While copyright exists automatically upon creation, enforcement requires registration.

Legal Advantages of Registration

Reason	Detail
Prerequisite for Lawsuits	Registration is required before filing a federal infringement lawsuit
Statutory Damages	Eligibility for damages up to $150,000 per willful infringement
Exclusive Rights Protection	Reproduction, distribution, performance, and derivative works

Objective 5.2: Learn HOW to Register Lyrics and Beats (U.S.)

Registration is completed online through the **Electronic Copyright Office (eCO)** system on the official U.S. Copyright Office website.

Objective 5.3: Identify the Two Works

Musical Work (Composition)

Protects lyrics, melody, and musical structure.

Sound Recording (Master)

Protects the final audio recording.

The Registration Process

1. **Prepare Deposit Copies**

    - Lyrics or audio for the composition

    - MP3 or WAV for the sound recording

2. **Select Application Type**

    - Use a single application when eligible

3. **Group Registration of Unpublished Works (GRUW)**

    - Register up to 10 unpublished songs cost-effectively

4. **Complete Application**

    - Enter titles, dates, authors, and claimants

5. **Pay the Fee**

    - Fees are nonrefundable

6. **Upload Deposits**

    - Submit digital files through the eCO system

Chapter 6: Setting Up Your Songtrust Account

Songtrust is a worldwide music publishing administration service. Its main purpose is to register your compositions internationally and collect **publishing royalties** (Performance and Mechanical) that your Performing Rights Organization (PRO) or the Mechanical Licensing Collective (MLC) often cannot collect outside your home territory.

As a **songwriter and producer**, you are essentially building an account for yourself as the creator and/or copyright owner of the musical composition.

Here is a step-by-step guide explaining how to set up and use your Songtrust account:

Step 1: Meet the Prerequisites

Before you sign up with Songtrust, you should have the following in place:

1. **PRO Affiliation:** You **must** be affiliated with a Performing Rights Organization (PRO) as a **Writer** in your home

country (e.g., ASCAP, BMI, SESAC in the US; SOCAN in Canada; PRS in the UK).

2. **Original Music:** You must own the copyright (or a percentage of the copyright) in the musical compositions you want to register.

3. **Music Released:** You should have at least one song distributed on a major platform.

Step 2: Create Your Songtrust Account

1. **Visit the Songtrust Website:** Go to the official Songtrust site and begin the sign-up process.

2. **Pay the Fee:** Songtrust typically charges a one-time, per-writer setup fee.

3. **Input Personal Details:** Provide your legal name, contact information, and payment details (how you want to be paid).

4. **Enter PRO Information:** This is critical. You will be asked for your PRO (e.g., BMI/ASCAP) and your unique **IPI/CAE number**. This number identifies you as a songwriter globally.

Step 3: Register Your Publishing Entity

As an independent songwriter/producer, you own the **Publisher's Share** (50%) of your composition.

- When you set up your PRO account, you may have created a "vanity publisher" entity (e.g., "My Music Publishing").

- Songtrust will act as the **administrator** for this publishing entity (or help you create one) and register it with collection societies worldwide.

- **ACTION:** Make sure your existing publishing name (if you have one) and the matching **Publisher IPI number** are correctly entered into your Songtrust account. This enables Songtrust to collect your **publisher's share** of royalties globally.

Step 4: Register Your Songs (Lyrics and Beats)

This is the most important step for you as a songwriter/producer. Every song, including your beats, must be registered individually.

1. **Add a New Song:** In your Songtrust dashboard, choose the option to **"Add a Song."**

2. **Enter Song Title:** Provide the main title and any alternate titles (if applicable).

3. **Input ISWC and ISRC Codes (If Available):**

   o **ISWC (International Standard Musical Work Code):** Identifies the **Composition** (the lyrics/beat). Your PRO or Songtrust will assign this after registration.

   o **ISRC (International Standard Recording Code):** Identifies the **Sound Recording** (the master audio file). Your distributor (e.g., TuneCore, DistroKid) assigns this when you release the music.

Tip for Producers: If you are a beat-maker, the composition is the underlying music, melody, and rhythm. The sound recording is the master track of the beat itself.

4. **Define Song Splits:** You must list **every co-writer and co-producer** who contributed to the **Composition** (lyrics and music/beat) and clearly define their percentage splits. **Splits must total 100%.**

As a Producer: If your contribution went beyond the master recording and included creating a key melody, chord progression, or musical hook, you are considered a co-writer and should have a split of the composition.

   o **Writers vs. Outside Writers:** List yourself (and any other Songtrust clients) as an **Account**

Writer. List collaborators who use a different administrator or collect directly from their PRO as an **Outside Writer**. Songtrust will only collect your share.

5. **Submit and Monitor:** Once you save and submit, Songtrust will verify the data and register the song with its network of global collection societies. You can track the status inside your account.

Important Note for Producers (Composition vs. Sound Recording)

Songtrust manages publishing royalties, which apply to the **composition** (lyrics and beat/music).

- **For the Beat/Music:** Make sure you are claiming a percentage in the **Music** authorship field during registration.

- **The Sound Recording:** The separate royalty generated by the sound recording is typically handled by your distributor and SoundExchange (for non-interactive digital radio). That is a separate process from Songtrust.

Chapter 7: Understanding Lease and Exclusive Agreements as a Producer

In the fast-moving world of music production, understanding the details of agreements is essential for producers and artists alike. This section explains the two main agreement types that govern the licensing of instrumental beats: the Lease Agreement (Non-Exclusive License) and the Exclusive Agreement (Exclusive License). By breaking down how each agreement works and outlining best practices for drafting them, producers can better navigate the real-world complexity of music licensing and protect their rights.

1. Lease Agreement (Non-Exclusive License)

A Lease Agreement, commonly called a Non-Exclusive License, is one of the most common and accessible agreements in the industry. It allows artists to use an instrumental track under specific, limited terms, which makes it ideal for independent and emerging musicians.

How a Lease Works

A Lease Agreement includes several core features that define how the license operates and what it means for both the producer and the artist.

Feature	Description
Exclusivity	**Non-Exclusive.** The producer retains full ownership and can license the same beat to other artists.
Cost	Low (typically **$20 - $200**), making it affordable for independent and emerging artists.
Usage Limits	**Limited.** The license is capped on commercial usage. Common limits include: **Streams/Sales:** e.g., max 100,000 digital streams. **Music Videos:** e.g., max 1 music video. **Performance:** e.g., max 50 live performances.
Duration	**Time-Bound.** Often 1 to 5 years, after which the artist must renew the lease or purchase an upgrade to continue distribution.
Ownership	**Producer** retains 100% of the beat's composition copyright. The artist owns the copyright to their lyrics and vocal performance.
Upgrade Path	Many producers allow the artist to **upgrade** to a higher-tier lease (e.g., an Unlimited Lease) or an Exclusive License if the song starts gaining traction.

Best Practices for Drafting a Lease

When drafting a Lease Agreement, clarity and detail are essential to avoid confusion and prevent disputes. Here are best practices to include:

1. **Clarity on Tiers:** If you offer multiple tiers (Basic, Premium, Unlimited), list the exact limits for each. An **"Unlimited Lease"** is a popular tier that removes stream and sales caps but *remains non-exclusive.*

2. **Credit Requirement:** The agreement must clearly state how the artist is required to credit the producer (e.g., "Produced by [Producer Name]"). This ensures the producer receives consistent recognition.

3. **Audio Quality:** Specify what the artist receives (e.g., MP3 for Basic, WAV for Premium, tracked-out stems for Unlimited). Higher-quality files support professional release standards.

4. **Content ID:** Address Content ID claims. Producers should either grant a Content ID license or clearly state that the artist's use is non-exclusive, to prevent false claims that interrupt the artist's YouTube or streaming monetization.

By following these practices, producers can create lease agreements that protect their interests while still giving artists the tools and clarity they need to move forward confidently.

2. Exclusive Agreement (Exclusive License)

In contrast, an Exclusive Agreement grants all commercial usage rights for the instrumental to one artist. This type of agreement is more detailed and typically comes with a higher price, because it involves a permanent transfer of exclusive commercial rights.

How an Exclusive Agreement Works

An Exclusive Agreement has key features that separate it from a lease.

Feature	Description
Exclusivity	**Exclusive.** The artist becomes the *sole owner* of the commercial usage rights for that instrumental.
Cost	High (typically **$300 - $5,000+**), reflecting the long-term exclusive commercial rights.
Usage Limits	**Unlimited.** No limits on streams, sales, performances, or music videos. The artist has full commercial freedom.
Duration	**Perpetual.** The rights last for the life of the copyright.
Ownership	**Producer retains** the original composition copyright (and the related **Writer's Share** of performance royalties). **Artist** receives ownership of the **Master Recording** of their completed song.
Publishing Split	The agreement defines the split of the **Publisher's Share** of royalties, which is often negotiated (e.g., 50% to Producer's Publisher, 50% to Artist's Publisher).

Best Practices for Drafting an Exclusive Agreement

Exclusive agreements require precise language so both parties fully understand the scope of rights and the long-term obligations. Best practices include:

1. **Transfer of Rights:** Clearly state that the producer is granting **Exclusive Master Use Rights** to the artist for the commercial recording. This ensures the artist understands the full scope of what they are purchasing.

2. **Removal Clause:** Include a mandatory clause requiring the producer to remove the beat from all online stores and platforms immediately after the exclusive sale. This protects the buyer's investment and supports true exclusivity.

3. **Stems/Files:** The producer should deliver the highest-quality master files and the **"stems"** (individual instrument tracks) for mixing and mastering. This helps the artist achieve a professional final release.

4. **Publishing and Royalties:** This is one of the most complex sections and must clearly define the **splits** for the *underlying composition*.

   - **Writer's Share:** The producer retains their agreed-upon percentage of the writer's share (e.g., 50% of the composition's writer's share).

- **Publisher's Share:** The publisher's share split must be clearly stated (often 50/50 between the producer's publisher and the artist's publisher).

5. **Previous Leases:** Include a **Notice of Outstanding Clients** clause. This informs the exclusive buyer that any artists who previously purchased a lease retain the right to use the beat until their existing lease terms end.

By applying these practices, producers can draft exclusive agreements that protect their rights while giving artists the confidence and security to release the track commercially.

Summary: Key Differences

Understanding the differences between lease agreements and exclusive agreements is essential for both producers and artists. Here is a quick comparison:

Feature	Lease Agreement (Non-Exclusive)	Exclusive Agreement
Rights Granted	Limited, temporary use of the instrumental under defined terms (rental-style license).	Unlimited, permanent commercial usage rights granted to one artist.
Producer's Beat	Can be licensed to multiple artists at the same time without restriction.	Must be permanently removed from sale and cannot be licensed again.
Master Recording Ownership	Typically owned by the artist who records vocals over the beat.	Owned exclusively by the artist who purchased the exclusive license.
Risk to Artist	Other artists may legally release songs using the same instrumental.	No competition, as no other artist can legally use the beat.
Best Use Case	Independent singles, mixtapes, demos, and early-stage releases.	High-priority singles, commercial releases, brand-focused projects, and long-term exploitation.

Chapter 8: Maximizing Your Streams Using AI as an Artist and Which LLC Is Best for You

In the constantly shifting music industry landscape, artists must evolve alongside emerging technologies and modern strategies in order to grow and remain competitive. This chapter explores actionable techniques for boosting streaming numbers, examines the growing influence of Artificial Intelligence (AI) in music creation, and explains how data-driven insights can be used to refine and strengthen your overall music strategy.

By the conclusion of this chapter, you will possess a well-rounded understanding of how to increase your music's exposure and build a sustainable, long-term career in today's digital ecosystem.

Tips for Increasing Stream Counts

Growing your stream counts is not simply a matter of uploading a track and waiting for results. Success requires a calculated approach that includes platform optimization, meaningful audience interaction, and consistent release activity. The strategies below are designed to help you navigate this competitive environment with intention and clarity.

Platform Optimization and Engagement

Strategy	Actionable Tip	Goal
Claim Your Profiles	Register and verify your artist profiles on **Spotify for Artists, Apple Music for Artists**, and **YouTube Studio**. Pitch your releases to official editorial playlists *before* launch through Spotify for Artists, and actively connect with independent playlist curators within your genre.	**Massive visibility** and expanded reach to new listeners.
Create Your Own Playlists	Develop mood-based or genre-focused playlists that blend your music with tracks from established artists. Promote these playlists across your social media channels to drive engagement.	**Fan loyalty** and **algorithmic lift**, as platforms reward traffic driven by artists.
Release Consistency	Maintain a predictable release cadence, such as one single every 6 to 8 weeks, to stay favored by platform algorithms and keep fans engaged.	**Ongoing relevance** and sustained algorithmic exposure.
Utilize Pre-Saves and Pre-Adds	Launch pre-save and pre-add campaigns to generate early activity, signaling strong demand to the algorithm on release day.	**Strong opening-day performance**, increasing chances of

		playlist place-ment.
Focus on Short-Form Video	Produce engaging, high-retention short-form videos for TikTok, Instagram Reels, and YouTube Shorts using your music. Apply a clear **Hook, Body, and Call to Action (CTA)** to direct viewers to full streams.	**New fan discovery** and **cross-platform traffic** to streaming links.

Streaming Mechanics: Best Practices

Understanding how streaming platforms measure engagement can directly impact performance. Keep the following mechanics in mind:

- **30-Second Rule:** A stream is generally counted only after a listener plays the track for at least **30 seconds**. Design your introduction to capture attention quickly and maintain interest beyond this mark.

- **No Muted Streams:** Streams played on mute are not counted. Encourage listeners to use headphones or keep volume at an audible level.

- **Playlist Saves Matter:** When a listener saves your track to their library or personal playlist, it sends a powerful signal to the algorithm that your music has long-term value.

Applying these practices helps establish a solid framework for increasing streams and growing your listener base.

Utilizing AI in Music Creation and Production

Artificial Intelligence is reshaping the music industry by offering artists advanced tools that enhance creativity and efficiency. Rather than replacing human expression, AI functions as a supportive collaborator, assisting artists in overcoming creative barriers and accelerating production workflows.

AI Applications in Music

AI Application	How It Works for the Artist	Benefits
Generative Music	AI systems generate melodies, chord structures, or full background tracks from text prompts such as "Lo-fi beat for studying in C minor."	**Creative stimulation** and rapid idea generation for compositions, jingles, or soundtracks.
Mixing and Mastering	AI mastering services analyze audio and apply compression, EQ, and limiting aligned with industry benchmarks within seconds.	**Time and cost efficiency**, delivering fast, professional-level demo masters.

Stem Separation	AI-powered tools isolate vocals, drums, and instruments from completed recordings.	**Simplified re-mixing,** cleaner sampling, and quick instrumental or acapella creation.
Lyrics and Vocal Generation	AI can draft lyrics around a theme or generate synthetic vocals with permission.	**Songwriting support** or placeholder vocals for instrumental creators.

Ethical and Legal Note: Always ensure that AI platforms guarantee copyright ownership of generated content and confirm that training data was obtained legally.

Integrating AI Into Your Workflow

Incorporating AI into your creative routine can provide substantial advantages. For example, when lyric writing stalls, AI-generated prompts can introduce fresh angles. Likewise, AI-driven mastering tools can reclaim hours of technical work, freeing you to focus on artistic direction.

That said, discernment is critical. AI should enhance, not override, your personal sound and identity. Treat AI as a creative partner rather than a replacement, and ensure every finished track reflects your artistic intent.

Leveraging Data and Analytics

In a data-driven industry, analytics function as a navigation system for your music career. Platforms like Spotify for Artists and Apple Music for Artists supply valuable metrics that inform both marketing decisions and creative direction.

Key Data Points to Track

Data Metric	What It Tells You	Strategic Action
Audience Demographics	Listener location, age range, and gender distribution.	**Targeted advertising** in top regions and **tour planning** based on fan concentration.
Source of Streams	Discovery sources such as playlists, libraries, and algorithmic features.	**Double down** on effective sources and reinforce algorithmic signals like saves and shares.
Skip and Retention Rate	How quickly listeners disengage from a track.	**Creative feedback** on intros and **mixing feedback** for albums with high skip rates.
Follower Conversion Rate	Percentage of listeners who become followers.	**Profile optimization**, including bios, visuals, and canvas content.
Most Popular Tracks	Songs with sustained or growing stream counts over time.	**Strategic focus** on high-performing releases.

Chapter 9: Music Registration and LLC Business Structure for Independent Artists

Within the evolving music industry, independent artists encounter both distinct challenges and valuable opportunities. Establishing a strong legal and operational foundation is essential to navigating this environment effectively. This section explores music registration, formal business structures, and professional management roles that support long-term success.

With a clear understanding of these components, independent artists can create sustainable careers and unlock multiple revenue pathways.

Registering Music: Operating as Both Label and Publisher

Independent artists must function in multiple roles. To succeed, you must operate simultaneously as a record label and a music publisher. This responsibility extends beyond creating music to ensuring every revenue source connected to that music is properly captured.

The Two Copyrights and Registration

Understanding the two core copyrights is fundamental. Each protects a different element of your work and must be registered correctly to secure full compensation.

Type of Copyright	What It Protects	Administered By	What You Need to Do
Sound Recording (Master)	The recorded performance itself.	**Record Label** (or you, if independent).	Assign an **ISRC** to each track through your distributor (DistroKid, TuneCore, etc.).
Musical Composition (Publishing)	Lyrics, melody, and chord structure.	**Music Publisher** (you, as an independent artist or LLC).	Register the work with a **PRO** such as **ASCAP**, **BMI**, or **SOCAN**.

The Role of the Independent Label

When you self-release, you assume full label responsibilities:

- **ISRC Acquisition:** Every recording requires an ISRC for tracking sales and streams.

- **Distributor Selection:** Choose a distributor that places your music on platforms like Spotify and Apple Music.

- **Metadata Accuracy:** Ensure consistent and accurate song information across all platforms to avoid royalty loss.

The Role of the Independent Publisher

As your own publisher, you manage all songwriting-related royalties:

- **PRO Registration:** Register as both writer and publisher to collect full performance royalties.

- **Mechanical Royalties:** Register with agencies such as **The MLC** in the U.S.

- **Split Sheets:** Document ownership percentages for all contributors to ensure clarity and fairness.

Executing these duties allows independent artists to operate professionally while maximizing income potential.

LLCs and Business Structures for Musicians

As income and expenses increase, forming a formal business entity becomes increasingly important. This protects personal assets and offers tax advantages.

Common Business Structures

Structure	Description	Pros	Cons
Sole Proprietorship	You and the business are legally the same entity.	Simple setup and minimal paperwork.	**No liability protection** for personal assets.
Limited Liability Company (LLC)	A separate legal entity from the owner.	Asset protection and tax flexibility.	Ongoing state fees and administrative upkeep.
Partnership	Two or more owners share responsibility.	Shared costs and formal operating agreements.	Partners often retain personal liability unless structured as an LLP.

Benefits of Forming an LLC

- **Liability Protection:** Shields personal assets from business-related legal claims.

- **Tax Deductions:** Allows legitimate business expenses to reduce taxable income.

- **Professional Credibility:** Enhances reputation when dealing with industry professionals.

Working With a Music Manager

As career demands grow, managing everything independently may become impractical. A music manager acts as the strategic leader of your career.

Manager Responsibilities

Key Function	Manager's Action
Career Strategy	Defines long-term goals and brand positioning.
Team Coordination	Oversees agents, publicists, lawyers, and business managers.
Business Development	Negotiates and evaluates deals.
Administration	Manages logistics, scheduling, and communication.
Networking	Leverages industry relationships to create opportunities.

When to Hire a Manager

- **Time Constraints:** Administrative demands interfere with creativity.

- **Career Complexity:** Multiple income streams require coordination.

- **Advocacy Needs:** Professional representation is required for negotiations.

Chapter 10: ALL MUSIC

Objectives:

1. Understand the importance of ALL MUSIC

2. Learn WHY you need your music in ALL MUSIC

3. Learn HOW to get your music in ALL MUSIC

The AllMusic Guide stands as one of the most respected and long-established music databases in the world. For artists and labels, having an AllMusic entry represents professional credibility and serves as a primary source of detailed industry data used across countless platforms.

Objective 10.1: Understanding the Importance of ALL MUSIC

Below is a detailed explanation of its significance, necessity, and submission structure.

AllMusic (formerly known as the All-Music Guide or AMG) is a U.S.-based online database that documents in-depth information on over three million albums, more than 30 million tracks, and countless artists. Unlike crowd-generated platforms,

AllMusic content is curated and maintained by a professional editorial staff.

Its database includes:

- **Detailed Recording Credits** including producers, engineers, and session musicians
- **Genre and Subgenre Classification**, covering both mainstream and highly niche categories

Data Licensing:

AllMusic's editorial content and metadata are licensed through its parent company, **TiVo** (formerly Rovi/Macrovision), to a wide range of third-party media platforms and digital services.

Music Discovery Engine:

With a classification system spanning more than 1,400 moods, genres, and stylistic tags, AllMusic intelligently links artists, albums, and musical movements. This makes it an indispensable resource for journalists, music historians, industry professionals, and fans seeking deeper musical context.

Objective 10.2: Why You Need Your Music in the ALL MUSIC Database

An AllMusic listing is essential for establishing an artist's professional footprint, discoverability, and industry recognition.

Why You Need It	Explanation
Professional Credibility	Being listed on AllMusic signals legitimacy within the music industry. Critics, journalists, radio programmers, and researchers frequently rely on AllMusic to confirm an artist's history and discography.
Industry Biographies	Many major DSPs and services, including **Spotify**, **iTunes/Apple Music**, and **Shazam**, source artist biographies and album reviews directly from AllMusic's licensed data feed. A professional bio on these platforms typically begins with AllMusic inclusion.
Complete Personnel Credits	AllMusic is considered the authoritative standard for documenting detailed session and technical credits, such as mixing engineers, mastering engineers, and instrumental contributors. This is especially critical for producers and session musicians who depend on verified credits.
Enhanced Search and Discovery	Accurate genre and stylistic classification helps distributors and licensees correctly categorize music, improving playlist placement, recommendation algorithms, and "similar artist" discovery.
Archival Importance	Inclusion permanently preserves your work within one of the most respected historical catalogs of recorded music.

Objective 10.3: How to Get Your Music in the ALL MUSIC Database

AllMusic submissions are not automatic and are never guaranteed. The platform prioritizes editorial integrity and data accuracy. Submissions are primarily handled through its data provider, **TiVo (formerly Rovi/Macrovision)**.

1. Submission Is Managed by a Third Party (TiVo/RhythmOne):

Artists do not submit directly to the AllMusic website. Instead, information is submitted to the content and data teams that license AllMusic material, generally through **TiVo/RhythmOne**.

2. Preferred Method: The "Product Submissions" Page:

AllMusic provides a dedicated **Product Submissions** page outlining how to submit content to its data provider.

The standard method usually requires emailing a highly detailed spreadsheet, often an Excel template, containing complete release metadata, including:

- Album Title and Artist Name

- UPC and ISRC codes

- Full track listing

- Official release date

- **Comprehensive credits**, covering all performers, producers, engineers, mixers, and songwriters with defined roles

- Artist biography written by the artist or label

For physical releases, a physical CD may still be requested in some cases, although digital submission is now more common.

4. Digital Distribution Integration (Indirect):

Digital distributors such as TuneCore or CD Baby deliver music to streaming platforms, but they **do not** automatically generate an AllMusic entry or biography. Distributors only provide basic metadata. Rich editorial content requires a direct submission to TiVo/RhythmOne for editorial review.

4. Editorial Review and Prioritization:

AllMusic's editorial team operates with a large backlog and evaluates submissions based on popularity, historical relevance, and industry demand. Even after submission, approval and publication may take several months or longer.

Conclusion:

Securing an AllMusic entry requires proactive, manual submission of complete and accurate metadata. While the process requires patience, inclusion is a major milestone in establishing a verified and enduring professional presence across the global music industry.

Chapter 11: APPLE MUSIC FOR ARTIST

Objectives:

1. Understand the importance of APPLE MUSIC FOR ARTIST

2. Learn WHY you need your music in APPLE MUSIC FOR ARTIST

3. Learn HOW to get your music in APPLE MUSIC FOR ARTIST

In the constantly evolving music industry, artists seek innovative methods to reach audiences, promote releases, and build sustainable brands. One of the most powerful tools available today is **Apple Music for Artists**. This platform not only hosts music but also delivers critical insights into listener behavior and performance data.

Objective 11.1: The Importance of Apple Music for Artists

Apple Music for Artists extends far beyond basic streaming functionality. It is a comprehensive artist management platform designed to support growth and strategy. With more than 88 million subscribers globally, Apple Music provides access to a massive audience. Its greatest value, however, lies in analytics and promotional tools that help artists understand their listeners and refine their marketing efforts.

Building Your Brand

In the digital era, branding is inseparable from music. Apple Music for Artists enables musicians to curate an artist profile featuring music, biography, images, and social links. This profile becomes a centralized destination where fans can explore and engage with the artist's identity. A polished and consistent profile strengthens visibility and attracts new listeners.

Objective 11.2: Why You Need Apple Music for Artists

Artists may question whether setting up and managing an Apple Music for Artists account is worth the effort. The advantages make the answer clear.

Increased Visibility

Apple Music is among the world's largest streaming platforms. Making music available here significantly increases discovery potential. Curated playlists, in particular, can drive major spikes in streams and followers, accelerating career momentum.

Access to Valuable Tools

The platform provides analytics dashboards and promotional tools that help artists navigate industry complexity. Features such as pre-save campaigns encourage early fan engagement, supporting stronger release-day performance.

Networking Opportunities

Apple Music for Artists can facilitate connections with other artists, producers, and industry professionals. Active engagement on the platform can uncover collaboration opportunities and strengthen professional relationships.

Monetization Potential

Through Apple Music, artists earn royalties based on streaming volume. While per-stream payouts are modest, consistent growth and audience expansion can generate meaningful revenue over time.

Objective 11.3: How to Get Your Apple Music for Artists Account Verified

Getting music onto Apple Music and gaining access to Apple Music for Artists are related but separate processes.

You **do not upload music directly** through Apple Music for Artists. The platform is used for analytics, profile management, and promotional assets.

Step 1: Distribute Your Music to Apple Music

All major streaming platforms require artists to work with a **digital music distributor**.

1. **Choose a Distributor:**
   Common options include:

   - **DistroKid**

   - **TuneCore**

   - **CD Baby**

   - **Symphonic**

   - **AWAL**

Apple Music also maintains a list of preferred distributors that meet quality standards.

2. **Upload Your Files:**
   Upload high-quality audio files, artwork (typically 3000 × 3000 pixels minimum), and complete metadata.

3. **Select Apple Music:**
   Ensure Apple Music and the iTunes Store are selected as distribution destinations.

4. **Delivery and Release:**
   Once fees are paid, the distributor submits your release to Apple. Music usually appears within days or weeks.

Your music must be live on Apple Music before proceeding to the next step.

Step 2: Claim Your Apple Music for Artists Profile

1. Visit **artists.apple.com** or download the Apple Music for Artists app.

2. Sign in using an Apple ID.

3. Request artist access and search for your live artist page.

4. Confirm ownership by selecting one of your official releases.

5. Choose your role and complete the application with detailed information.

6. Wait for approval, which may take some time.

Step 3: Manage Your Profile and Music

Once approved, you can:

- Upload a professional artist image

- Submit lyrics

- Monitor analytics and listener demographics

- Create promotional assets

- Manage profile information

Conclusion:

Apple Music for Artists is an essential platform for modern musicians. By understanding its value, leveraging its tools, and following the proper verification process, artists can expand reach, strengthen branding, and make informed strategic decisions. When used consistently, the platform becomes a powerful driver of long-term career growth.

Chapter 12: Spotify for Artists

Objectives:

1. Understand the importance of using SPOTIFY FOR ARTISTS

2. Learn WHY you need SPOTIFY FOR ARTISTS

3. Learn HOW to get your SPOTIFY FOR ARTISTS account verified and music added

In today's rapidly evolving music industry, the digital ecosystem has become an essential space for artists to present their work, engage directly with fans, and develop long-term careers. Among the wide range of streaming platforms available, Spotify remains a dominant force, serving hundreds of millions of listeners worldwide and hosting one of the most expansive music libraries in existence.

For artists, learning how to properly use **Spotify for Artists** is no longer optional. It is a foundational tool that supports visibility, strategic growth, and informed decision-making. This section explores why Spotify for Artists matters, why every musician should take advantage of it, and the precise steps required to verify an account and ensure music is correctly delivered to the platform.

Objective 12.1: The Importance of Using Spotify for Artists

A Gateway to Global Exposure

As streaming has become the primary mode of music consumption, Spotify has established itself as a leading discovery platform. With hundreds of millions of active users, including a substantial premium subscriber base, Spotify provides artists with access to a truly global audience.

For emerging musicians, this reach eliminates the geographical limitations that once restricted exposure. A track released on Spotify can be discovered by listeners across continents within hours of release. One of the most powerful advantages of Spotify for Artists is the depth of analytical data it provides. Artists gain access to detailed listener information, including age demographics, geographic locations, and listening behaviors.

This data is invaluable. By studying listener trends, artists can make smarter decisions regarding tour locations, promotional strategies, and merchandise offerings. Informed decisions lead to more efficient marketing and stronger overall career outcomes.

Enhanced Fan Engagement

Spotify for Artists offers tools that allow musicians to interact more directly with their audience. Artists can share announcements, post behind-the-scenes updates, and curate playlists that reflect their inspirations and influences. This type of interaction builds familiarity and trust, strengthening the bond between artist and listener.

In a digital environment where authenticity matters, Spotify for Artists provides musicians with the resources needed to foster long-term fan loyalty.

Playlist Placement

Placement on Spotify playlists remains one of the most effective ways to increase visibility and streaming numbers. Spotify for Artists enables artists to submit unreleased tracks for editorial playlist consideration. This process significantly increases the likelihood of being featured on playlists that introduce music to new audiences at scale.

Playlists often serve as the primary entry point for listeners discovering new artists. Their influence on growth and exposure cannot be overstated.

Objective 12.2: Why You Need Spotify for Artists

Building Your Brand

Brand identity is a critical element of success in the modern music landscape. Spotify for Artists allows musicians to craft a professional artist profile that reflects their unique image and story. From updating biographies to selecting profile visuals, the platform enables artists to present themselves intentionally and cohesively.

A well-designed profile helps establish credibility and leaves a strong impression on fans, curators, and industry professionals.

Monetization Opportunities

Although Spotify does not issue direct per-stream payments outside of standard royalty distribution, it plays a major role in opening revenue pathways. A growing listener base can attract interest from labels, booking agents, sponsors, and licensing opportunities. Additionally, increased exposure on Spotify often leads to higher merchandise sales and greater demand for live performances.

Networking and Collaboration

Spotify for Artists also functions as a professional ecosystem. Artists can discover peers, producers, and collaborators, creating opportunities for creative partnerships. Relationships remain a driving force in the music industry, and Spotify for Artists makes these connections more accessible.

Staying Relevant

Maintaining relevance requires consistent updates and engagement. Spotify for Artists allows musicians to highlight new releases, announce upcoming shows, and share important career milestones. An active and updated profile keeps artists visible and top-of-mind for listeners.

Objective 12.3: How to Get Your Spotify for Artists Account Verified and Music Added

Step 1: Create Your Spotify for Artists Account

Begin by visiting the Spotify for Artists website and selecting "Get Access." Existing Spotify users can log in using their current credentials and convert their account into an artist profile.

Step 2: Claim Your Profile

After logging in, artists must claim their profile by verifying their identity. This includes submitting the artist name, associated email address, and links to official social media accounts. This step ensures profile security and authorized management.

Step 3: Verify Your Account

Verification establishes trust and authenticity. Artists must provide details about their music catalog, social platforms, and achievements. Once approved, the profile receives a blue verification badge, confirming legitimacy to listeners.

Step 4: Upload Your Music

Music cannot be uploaded directly through Spotify for Artists. Instead, artists must use a digital distributor such as DistroKid, TuneCore, or CD Baby. These services deliver music to Spotify and other streaming platforms.

Step 5: Promote Your Music

Once tracks are live, artists should actively promote releases using Spotify for Artists tools. Sharing music on social platforms, collaborating with other artists, and pitching songs to playlists all contribute to broader reach.

Step 6: Analyze Your Data

Spotify for Artists provides robust analytics covering streams, audience demographics, and engagement patterns. Reviewing this data allows artists to adjust marketing strategies and plan future releases more effectively.

Step 7: Engage with Your Fans

Ongoing engagement is essential. Artists should share updates, interact with listeners, and create playlists that reflect their creative journey. Strong artist-fan relationships are the foundation of sustainable success.

Conclusion

Spotify for Artists is a vital resource for musicians navigating the digital music economy. By understanding its value, utilizing its tools, and following the verification and release process, artists can unlock meaningful growth opportunities. From global exposure to data-driven decision-making, Spotify for Artists empowers musicians to take ownership of their careers and compete effectively in an evolving industry.

Chapter 13: SOUNDSCAN

Objectives:

1. Understand the importance of SOUNDSCAN

2. Learn WHY you need your music in the SOUNDSCAN database

3. Learn HOW to get your music in the SOUNDSCAN database

In the modern music industry, where digital streaming and physical sales coexist, success is increasingly measured by data. One of the most influential systems in this space is SOUNDSCAN, which tracks music sales across multiple platforms. This chapter explains why SOUNDSCAN matters, why artists and labels must ensure their music is included, and how to properly register releases within the system.

Objective 13.1: The Importance of Using SOUNDSCAN

The Pulse of the Industry

SOUNDSCAN functions as the backbone of music sales reporting. Since its establishment in 1989, it has supplied the data that shapes charts, sales reports, and industry trends. For artists, producers, and labels, SOUNDSCAN acts as a navigational tool in an otherwise complex market.

Chart placements derived from SOUNDSCAN data are widely regarded as benchmarks of success. When an album appears on Billboard charts, it reflects not only artistic effort but also effective distribution and marketing execution. This visibility often leads to touring opportunities, brand partnerships, and increased industry attention.

Data-Driven Decisions

SOUNDSCAN equips artists and labels with reliable sales data that supports strategic planning. By examining sales performance, artists can identify which releases resonate most with listeners. This insight allows for better-informed decisions regarding future projects and promotional investments.

Objective 13.2: Why You Need SOUNDSCAN

The Competitive Edge

In an oversaturated market, insight is power. SOUNDSCAN data helps artists recognize trends and identify market gaps. If a specific genre or release format gains traction, artists can adapt their strategies to align with demand and remain competitive.

Building a Fanbase

Sales data also reveals where music performs best geographically. Artists can use this information to prioritize tour locations and focus promotional efforts where engagement is strongest. Understanding audience demographics ensures that marketing resources are used efficiently.

Securing Partnerships and Funding

Verified sales data strengthens an artist's credibility when seeking investors, sponsors, or collaborators. Demonstrating measurable performance builds confidence among stakeholders and increases the likelihood of financial support.

Objective 13.3: How to Get Your UPC Added to SOUNDSCAN

Understanding UPCs

A UPC (Universal Product Code) is a unique identifier assigned to a music release. It allows retailers and distributors to track sales accurately. Without a UPC, sales cannot be properly recorded by SOUNDSCAN.

Step 1: Obtain a UPC

UPCs can be acquired through:

- **GS1:** The official source for UPCs, offering the most reliable registration.

- **Digital Distributors:** Platforms such as DistroKid, TuneCore, and CD Baby often provide UPCs as part of their distribution services.

Step 2: Register with SOUNDSCAN

Once a UPC is secured, artists must register it with SOUND-SCAN by submitting release details.

Registration Process:

1. Visit the **Luminate Google Form**

2. Complete the form with accurate information, including UPC, artist name, album title, release date, and label de-tails.

3. Submit the form for processing and approval.

Accuracy is essential, as errors can delay tracking or prevent in-clusion.

Step 3: Monitor Your Sales

After registration, artists should regularly review sales data through the SOUNDSCAN system. Monitoring performance en-ables timely marketing adjustments and informed release plan-ning.

Step 4: Promote Your Release

With tracking in place, promotion becomes critical. Artists

should leverage social media, email campaigns, and live performances to drive sales. Increased activity enhances both revenue and chart visibility.

Conclusion

SOUNDSCAN is more than a reporting tool. It is a foundational system that validates success and informs strategic decisions. By understanding its role, ensuring proper registration, and actively monitoring performance, artists and labels gain clarity in a competitive marketplace. Every sale contributes to long-term growth, and with SOUNDSCAN properly configured, artists are better positioned to advance their careers with confidence.

Chapter 14: GS1 Barcodes

Objectives:

1. Understand the importance of GS1 BARCODES

2. Learn WHY you need GS1 BARCODES

3. Learn HOW to set up your account and order merchandise BARCODES

GS1 barcodes are the internationally accepted standard for product identification and are a foundational requirement for any business intending to sell merchandise through brick-and-mortar retailers, online marketplaces, or structured supply chains. They enable consistent product recognition across global commerce systems.

Objective 14.1: Understanding the Importance of GS1 Barcodes

A GS1 barcode, such as a UPC or EAN, visually represents a **Global Trade Item Number (GTIN)**. This number functions as a permanent, unique digital identifier for a specific product, acting as its fingerprint in commercial databases.

GS1 Standard	Description
Global Trade Item Number (GTIN)	The unique numerical identifier assigned to each product and encoded beneath the barcode.
GS1 Company Prefix	A company-specific identifier issued by GS1 that forms the beginning of all GTINs you generate, officially identifying you as the brand owner.

Key Benefits

Global Standardized Communication:

GS1 standards establish a universal "business language." This shared framework allows product data to be accurately scanned, exchanged, and interpreted by retailers, distributors, and logistics partners worldwide without ambiguity or error.

Retail and E-commerce Acceptance:

Nearly all major retailers and online marketplaces, including Amazon, Walmart, Google Shopping, and eBay, either require or strongly prefer GS1-issued barcodes. Products using codes not licensed to the seller are frequently rejected or delisted.

Traceability and Inventory Control:

GS1 barcodes significantly improve supply chain efficiency by enabling:

- Rapid, error-free checkout scanning

- Precise inventory tracking across locations

- Faster and more targeted product recalls when necessary

Brand Credibility and Anti-Counterfeiting:

Obtaining barcodes directly from GS1 verifies that you are the legitimate brand owner. Retailers routinely cross-check GTINs against the GS1 database, protecting your brand from counterfeit listings and unauthorized code reuse.

Objective 14.2: Why You Need GS1 Barcodes

Authentic GS1 barcodes are essential if your business intends to sell merchandise in the following contexts:

Necessity	Why It's Required
Selling in Traditional Retail Stores	Point-of-Sale systems are configured to recognize GS1-compliant GTINs. Products without valid GS1 barcodes are typically refused by retailers.
Selling on Major E-commerce Platforms	Marketplaces rely on GTINs to authenticate listings, group identical products, and prevent fraud. Using unlicensed codes can lead to listing removal or account penalties.
Managing a Growing Product Line	Every unique product variation, such as size or color differences, requires its own distinct GTIN for accurate tracking and reporting.

Scaling Your Supply Chain	GS1 standards support identifiers for cases, pallets, and physical locations through systems like the **Global Location Number (GLN)**, which distributors and wholesalers require.

Objective 14.3: How to Set Up Your Account and Order Barcodes

Authentic GS1 barcodes are obtained by registering with your country's official GS1 Member Organization.

Step 1: Determine How Many Barcodes You Need

This decision directly affects your licensing cost.

- **Rule:** Each unique product variation requires a separate GTIN.

- **Example:** A T-shirt offered in **3 sizes (S, M, L)** and **3 colors (Red, Blue, Green)** requires **3 × 3 = 9 barcodes.**

Step 2: Choose Your License Type

License Type	Best For	Cost Structure
Single GTIN (UPC)	Businesses with one or very few products and no expansion plans.	One-time fee per barcode with no annual renewal.

GS1 Company Prefix	Businesses planning to expand product lines or require additional GS1 identifiers.	Initial license fee based on barcode capacity plus an annual renewal fee.

Step 3: Purchase Your License

1. **Locate Your Local GS1 Office:** Visit your country's official GS1 website.

2. **Apply and Pay:** Select your license type and complete the application.

3. **Receive Your Prefix or GTIN:** Upon approval, GS1 issues your company prefix or individual GTINs immediately.

Step 4: Create and Manage Your Barcodes

1. **Access the GS1 Data Hub:** Included with your membership.

2. **Assign GTINs:** Enter product details such as brand name, description, and net content.

3. **Generate Barcode Images:** Download high-resolution barcode files suitable for packaging and print.

4. **Go to Market:** Your product is now officially and globally identifiable.

Chapter 15: NIELSEN BDS

In the modern music industry, precise and unbiased airplay data is critical. As artists and professionals attempt to measure radio impact and chart performance, **NIELSEN BDS** remains a foundational reference point. Although ownership and technology have evolved, its core purpose remains unchanged: accurate airplay measurement.

Objective 15.1: Understanding the Importance of NIELSEN BDS (Luminate/Mediabase)

Originally known as **Nielsen Broadcast Data Systems**, NIELSEN BDS has long been the industry benchmark for tracking radio and broadcast airplay. Today, its data operations are owned by **Luminate**, while real-time airplay monitoring is powered by **Mediabase**.

The Role of NIELSEN BDS

Billboard Chart Calculations:

NIELSEN BDS airplay data is a major component in determining **Billboard** chart rankings, including the **Hot 100** and genre-specific airplay charts. Chart performance remains a primary indicator of commercial success.

Performance Royalty Distribution:

Performance Rights Organizations such as BMI, ASCAP, and SESAC depend on BDS data to allocate performance royalties accurately. Without reliable tracking, royalty payments would lack fairness and precision.

Industry Strategy and Promotion:

Labels, promoters, managers, and programmers analyze BDS data to:

- Measure campaign effectiveness
- Allocate promotional budgets
- Identify markets for touring and radio focus

Fraud Elimination:

Prior to automated monitoring, radio stations self-reported playlists, leaving room for manipulation. NIELSEN BDS introduced continuous digital pattern recognition, ensuring objective, verifiable airplay data.

Objective 15.2: Why You Need NIELSEN BDS Tracking

Artists and rights holders must ensure their music is encoded for two core reasons: **validation** and **compensation.**

Chart Eligibility:

Unencoded tracks do not count toward official airplay charts, regardless of how often they are played.

Royalty Collection:

PROs rely on BDS data to determine when and where music is broadcast. Unregistered recordings are effectively invisible, resulting in lost income.

Credibility and Leverage:

Verified spin counts strengthen negotiating power with promoters, booking agents, managers, and sponsors, directly impacting career growth.

Objective 15.3: How You Submit to NIELSEN BDS (Luminate/Mediabase)

To ensure tracking, artists must submit directly to **Mediabase.**

Required Identifiers:

- **ISRC** for the recording

- **UPC or GTIN** for the release

Digital Submission Process (Recommended)

1. **Prepare Identifiers:** Confirm ISRC and UPC/GTIN accuracy.

2. **Complete Mediabase New Music Notification:** Submit metadata, upload audio, and select radio formats.

3. **Audio Encoding:** A unique digital fingerprint is created for monitoring systems.

4. **Verify Submission Links:** Always confirm current submission requirements through official Luminate or Mediabase resources.

Conclusion

NIELSEN BDS, operating through Luminate and Mediabase, remains an essential infrastructure tool in the music industry. Proper understanding, accurate submission, and diligent tracking ensure artists receive recognition, chart placement, and rightful compensation in a data-driven marketplace.

Chapter 16: Music Reports

In the constantly shifting music industry landscape, having a clear grasp of how rights administration and royalty distribution function is essential for songwriters, composers, and music publishers. One of the most influential organizations operating within this ecosystem is **Music Reports, Inc. (MRI)**. Acting as a critical intermediary, MRI supports licensing accuracy and royalty payment integrity across digital platforms and music users.

This section examines the role Music Reports plays within the industry, explains why registration with MRI is vital, and outlines how to ensure your music is properly submitted to their system.

Objective 16.1: Understanding the Importance of Music Reports (MRI)

Music Reports, Inc. is far more than another data entity in the music business. It is a foundational pillar of modern rights administration. As the operator of **Songdex**, the world's largest independent music rights registry, MRI ensures that composers and publishers receive the royalties rightfully owed to them.

Key Roles of the Music Reports Licensing Platform

At the core of MRI's operations is its sophisticated licensing infrastructure. Music Reports works closely with major digital service providers (DSPs) and a wide range of music users, including streaming services, fitness platforms, and broadcasters. Global companies such as Amazon, Pandora, and Microsoft rely on MRI to fulfill their music licensing responsibilities.

MRI functions as a central pipeline for usage data and financial reporting. When music is streamed, broadcast, or otherwise utilized, Music Reports receives detailed play logs from its clients. Using this information, MRI references the Songdex database to calculate royalty allocations with precision. This workflow is essential to guaranteeing that songwriters and publishers are compensated accurately and transparently.

Data Hub: Songdex

Songdex is MRI's proprietary metadata repository and serves as a comprehensive archive of composition information. The database stores critical data points such as songwriter identities, publisher affiliations, ownership percentages, and rights splits for millions of musical works.

This depth of data allows compositions to be correctly matched to sound recordings, ensuring payments reach the proper rights holders. Without this level of granularity, royalty processing errors and unclaimed income would increase substantially.

Objective 16.2: Why You Need to Register with Music Reports

For songwriters and publishers, enrolling with Music Reports, specifically through the Songdex Registry, is not optional. It is a fundamental requirement for safeguarding royalty income.

Below are the primary reasons registration is necessary:

Why You Need to Register	Explanation
Collect Mechanical Royalties	Music Reports administers mechanical licensing and payments for many international digital services. Registration in Songdex is required to receive these royalties.
Claim Unmatched Royalties	Songdex enables creators to locate and claim compositions with unidentified ownership, commonly known as "black box" royalties.
Direct Licensing Opportunities	Registration allows you to opt into voluntary direct licenses covering mechanical, synchronization, and sometimes performance rights.
Accurate Royalty Payments	Major platforms depend on Songdex metadata. Accurate ISWC data, ownership splits, and contact details ensure faster, error-free payouts.
Synchronization Royalty Support	MRI assists in tracking and administering music used in visual media, including broadcast and streaming television content.

Failing to register exposes songwriters and publishers to unnecessary financial risk. Unclaimed royalties and incorrect data entries can result in lost income that may never be recovered.

Chapter 17: Understanding and Utilizing MEDIABASE

Objectives

1. Understand the importance of MEDIABASE

2. Learn why MEDIABASE is essential

3. Learn how to submit music to MEDIABASE

In today's competitive music industry, artists and labels must leverage accurate data to succeed. One of the most powerful tools available is **Mediabase**, the leading radio airplay monitoring and charting service across the United States and Canada. This section explains Mediabase's function, why it matters, and how to ensure your music is properly tracked.

Objective 17.1: Understanding the Importance of MEDIABASE

Mediabase is not a music catalog or library. It is a subscription-based analytics engine that drives radio strategy across the industry. Its data directly influences artist careers, programming decisions, and label promotion efforts.

Key Roles of Mediabase

Radio Airplay Tracking

Mediabase monitors over 1,800 radio stations spanning more than 160 markets. Using proprietary detection technology, it identifies every verified spin a registered track receives. This tracking provides artists and labels with precise insight into reach, growth, and audience exposure.

Chart Compilation

Mediabase data fuels its highly influential weekly charts, covering nearly every radio format including Top 40, Country, Rock, Urban, and more. Chart placement significantly boosts visibility and can trigger increased airplay, media attention, and booking opportunities.

Industry Benchmark

Mediabase charts are published weekly in outlets such as *Pollstar* and are frequently referenced by radio countdown shows and music industry media. This widespread usage solidifies Mediabase as a trusted industry standard.

Objective 17.2: Why You Need Your Music Tracked by MEDIABASE

Mediabase tracking is not optional for artists pursuing radio success. It is a prerequisite.

Chart Eligibility

For songs to appear on respected radio airplay charts, including those influencing *Billboard* methodologies, they must be detected by Mediabase. Without tracking, radio success cannot be officially recognized.

Radio Promotion Tool

Radio programmers, music directors, and promotion teams rely on Mediabase to:

1. Monitor songs currently in rotation

2. Identify emerging trends and rising artists

3. Make informed decisions about playlist additions

This makes Mediabase indispensable for breaking or sustaining radio momentum.

Credibility for Booking and Deals

Verified Mediabase airplay data strengthens negotiations with booking agents, managers, promoters, and labels. Airplay statistics translate directly into perceived commercial value.

Data-Driven Strategy

Mediabase reports show exactly where and when tracks are played. Artists can focus promotional efforts on high-performing regions and formats for maximum return.

Royalty Verification

Airplay data contributes to performance royalty calculations by PROs such as ASCAP, BMI, and SESAC, reinforcing Mediabase's role in accurate compensation.

Objective 17.3: How You Submit to MEDIABASE

Proper submission ensures Mediabase can recognize your song each time it airs.

Step 1: Obtain Required Codes

- **ISRC:** A unique 12-character code identifying the specific recording

- **UPC:** Identifies the release product (single or album)

Step 2: Use the New Music Notification System

Submit your release using Mediabase's **New Music Notification** form. Required details include:

- Artist name, song title, and label/imprint

- ISRC and UPC codes

- Official release date

- Target radio formats

Step 3: Provide the Audio File for Encoding

Mediabase encodes your track with an inaudible digital watermark, allowing detection during broadcasts. Instructions for file upload or physical delivery are provided during submission.

Step 4: Follow Up and Verify

A song appears in Mediabase reports only after its first monitored airplay.

- Independent artists must still pursue radio promotion separately

- Subscribers or promoters can verify encoding status once airplay is detected

- Non-subscribers may contact the Mediabase Support or Discrepancy Desk for confirmation

Conclusion

Mediabase is an indispensable asset for artists and labels targeting radio exposure. Understanding its function, ensuring your music is properly tracked, and following the correct submission steps can significantly elevate your career. In an industry driven by data, Mediabase remains a critical gateway to radio success and long-term growth.

Chapter 18: Gracenotes – The Unsung Hero of Music Metadata

Objectives:

1. Understand the importance of GRACENOTES

2. Learn WHY you need your music in the Gracenotes Database

3. Learn HOW to get your music in the Gracenotes Database

The **Gracenote Database** is a foundational element of today's music ecosystem. It plays a critical role in ensuring that your music is accurately identified and properly delivered to listeners across countless platforms, devices, and listening environments.

Below is a structured breakdown of its importance, why it is necessary, and how the submission process works.

Objective 18.1: Understanding the Importance of GRACENOTE

Gracenote (a Nielsen company) is the world's leading provider of entertainment metadata and content-recognition technology. Its system functions as a massive, centralized repository containing verified information for millions of music recordings worldwide.

Key Functions and Technologies:

CD Recognition (CDDB):

Gracenote originated as the **CD Database (CDDB)**. When a commercial audio CD is inserted into a computer, music software applications (such as iTunes/Apple Music, Windows Media Player, and other media players) analyze the disc's track lengths to generate a unique digital signature. That signature is then matched against the Gracenote database to retrieve the correct song titles, artist names, and album information.

Audio Fingerprinting:

For digital audio files, streaming platforms, and radio broadcasts, Gracenote relies on advanced **acoustic fingerprinting** technology. This process creates a unique digital identifier based on the actual sound of the recording. Even if text-based metadata is missing, incomplete, or corrupted, the fingerprint allows systems to correctly recognize the track.

Rich Metadata:

Beyond basic song and artist details, Gracenote supplies deep, descriptive metadata, including:

- Album artwork

- Genre and sub-genre classifications

- Mood and tempo indicators

- Era and geographic origin

Discovery and Personalization

This rich metadata fuels search functionality, music discovery tools, and personalized recommendations across major streaming services, smart devices, and in-car entertainment systems.

Objective 18.2: Why You Need Your Music in the Gracenote Database

Submitting your music to the Gracenote database ensures that your work is **recognizable, searchable, and professionally displayed**, no matter how or where a listener encounters it.

Why You Need It	Explanation
Consumer-Friendly Presentation (CDs)	If your CD is not registered, tracks will appear as generic labels such as **"Track 01"** or **"Track 02"** when inserted into a computer. This looks unprofessional, frustrates listeners, and prevents proper music organization. Registration ensures accurate titles and artist information display automatically.
In-Car Systems & Smart Devices	Vehicle audio systems, smart speakers (Alexa, Google Home), and premium home audio equipment depend on Gracenote to display cover art, track data, and enable voice commands like "Play the song 'X' by 'Y.'" Without Gracenote, devices may fail to identify or play your music correctly.

Enhanced Discovery	Streaming platforms use Gracenote's detailed metadata (mood, tempo, style) to build algorithmic playlists and radio stations. Proper registration ensures your music is categorized accurately and recommended to listeners searching for a specific **"vibe"** or **"style."**
Metadata Consistency	Gracenote acts as a centralized "source of truth" for your music's identity, reducing errors, misspellings, and conflicting data across platforms.

Objective 18.3: How to Get Your Music in the Gracenote Database

The submission method depends on whether your release is physical or digital.

A. For Physical CDs (Primary Method)

This traditional process uses the CD's unique **Table of Contents (TOC)** signature.

1. **Finalize the CD Master:**
   Ensure all track lengths are final, as the digital signature is derived from timing.

2. **Use CD-R/RW Software (such as iTunes/Apple Music):**

   - Insert your final, commercial-ready CD into your computer.

- Open iTunes or the Apple Music app on macOS. The software will attempt to identify the CD and may display generic track names.

- **Manually Enter Data:** Select all tracks and input the correct **Artist Name, Album Title, Track Titles**, and related metadata.

- **Submit to Gracenote:** Use the menu option labeled **"Submit CD Track Names"** or **"Submit Album Information."**

3. **Wait for Processing:**

   Once submitted, the information is reviewed and processed by Gracenote. Approval and global propagation typically take several days to a few weeks.

B. For Digital Distribution (Most Common Today)

For digital releases, your distributor usually handles the Gracenote connection.

1. **Use an Aggregator/Distributor:**

   Most major distributors (TuneCore, DistroKid, CD Baby, etc.) include Gracenote submission as part of their standard distribution services.

2. **Ensure Metadata Accuracy:**

   When uploading your release, verify that all metadata (artist name, track title, ISRC, genre, and artwork) is

100% accurate and complete. Errors submitted at this stage will carry directly into the Gracenote database.

Conclusion

If you sell physical CDs, submit track names manually through a program like iTunes or Apple Music. For digital releases, confirm that your distributor includes Gracenote submission and always review your metadata carefully before release.

Chapter 19: Navigating The MLC: A Guide for Self-Published Song-writers

This course equips self-published songwriters with essential knowledge about the **Mechanical Licensing Collective (The MLC)**, its role within the royalty ecosystem, and the steps required to ensure proper collection of U.S. digital mechanical royalties. Participants will learn how to navigate the MLC system effectively and maximize earnings from streaming platforms.

Target Audience:

- Beginner self-published songwriters

- Independent musicians seeking clarity on the MLC

Objectives:

1. Understand the importance of MLC

2. Learn WHY you need MLC

3. Learn HOW to get your music into MLC

Objective 19.1: Understand the Importance of MLC

As an independent creator, you operate in two roles simultaneously: **the Songwriter** (creative contributor) and **the Publisher** (copyright administrator).

The **MLC (Mechanical Licensing Collective)** is essential because it is the **only organization authorized to administer U.S. digital mechanical royalties,** allowing you to properly fulfill your publisher role.

🎧 The MLC: Serving the Songwriter and the Publisher

Role	Responsibility to the Composition	Royalties Collected	Collecting Organization (U.S.)
Songwriter (Writer Share)	Writing lyrics and melody	Performance royalties (50% of public performance income)	Your **PRO** (ASCAP, BMI, etc.)
Publisher (Publisher Share)	Owning and administering the copyright	Digital mechanical royalties (reproduction income from streams)	**The MLC**

1. The MLC as the Publisher's Tool

Each U.S. stream generates a **digital mechanical royalty**, which is legally categorized as a publisher royalty. Your PRO does **not** collect this income.

The problem before The MLC:

Independent publishers had to license and collect from every DSP individually, an unrealistic process.

The solution:

The U.S. government created The MLC as the **exclusive administrator** of a blanket license covering all U.S. digital mechanical rights. Streaming services pay these royalties directly to The MLC.

Why this matters:

If you do not register with The MLC, your publisher royalties remain **unmatched and unpaid**, as The MLC cannot distribute funds without verified membership and work registration.

2. The MLC as the Songwriter's Advocate

For self-published songwriters who retain full publishing ownership, The MLC offers a direct and cost-free collection path.

- **Free Service:** The MLC is funded by DSPs and charges no commission.

- **Transparency:** Members access a portal to register works and verify data.

- **Historical Royalties:** The MLC distributes billions in previously unmatched mechanical royalties. Membership allows you to claim your share.

🔑 Your Action Steps (Wearing Both Hats)

Step	Role & Action	Key Data Required
1. Sign Up	**Publisher Role:** Create a Member Account as a "Self-Administered Songwriter"	IPI/CAE number
2. Register Works	**Songwriter Role:** Register compositions and writer splits	Writer splits totaling 100%
3. Claim Publishing	**Publisher Role:** Claim 100% of the publisher share	ISRC from distributor

Objective 19.2: Why You Need The MLC

The MLC is the **only entity authorized to collect U.S. streaming mechanical royalties**, which your PRO and distributor do not handle.

Three Core Reasons:

1. **Your PRO Does Not Collect Mechanical Royalties**

   - Performance royalties: collected by PROs

   - Mechanical royalties: collected only by **The MLC** in the U.S.

2. **Access to Historical Unmatched Royalties**

   Billions in unclaimed royalties are being researched and distributed by The MLC. Proper registration enables recovery of past earnings.

3. **Free and Transparent**

   - No membership fees

   - 100% payout distribution

   - Public searchable database for verification

Conclusion

The MLC is non-negotiable for collecting U.S. digital mechanical royalties.

Objective 19.3: Learn HOW to Get Your Music in MLC

🛠️ Phase 1: Becoming an MLC Member

1. Visit The MLC website and select **"Connect to Collect."**

2. Create a user profile for identity verification.

3. Establish a **Member Account** (Self-Administered Songwriter or Publisher).

4. Add your **IPI/CAE number** from your PRO.

5. Submit for approval (typically 1–3 business days).

🎧 Phase 2: Registering Your Works

Step 1: Search First

Use the Claiming Tool to locate existing registrations.

Step 2: Register the Work

Data Point	Description	Source
Song Title	Exact composition name	Your records
Writers & Splits	Legal names and ownership percentages (100%)	Split sheets
Publishers & Shares	Member Account and ownership	MLC account
IPI/CAE Numbers	All writers and publishers	PRO records

Step 3: Add ISRC (Recommended)

Links the sound recording to the composition.

Step 4: Review and Submit

Confirm all data accuracy before submission.

Conclusion

By registering with The MLC, self-published songwriters ensure they are fully compensated for U.S. digital mechanical royalties and gain access to both current and historical revenue streams.

Chapter 20: YOUR Countries Accounts 🌍

I. PERFORMANCE RIGHTS ORGANIZATIONS

The music rights collection universe is international, and almost every country has its own version of a **Performance Rights Organization (PRO)**, often described more broadly as a **Collective Management Organization (CMO)**.

These societies are connected through **Reciprocal Agreements**, which allow your home PRO (such as ASCAP or BMI) to collect your performance royalties when your song is played in other countries.

Below is a snapshot of major PROs/CMOs worldwide, grouped by region:

🌍 International Performance Rights Organizations (PROs)

Region	Country	PRO/CMO Name(s)	Key Notes
North America	United States	**ASCAP, BMI, SESAC, Global Music Rights (GMR)**	Multiple major PROs; The MLC handles U.S. digital mechanicals.

North America	Canada	**SOCAN** (Society of Composers, Authors and Music Publishers of Canada)	Main collecting society for performance and publishing in Canada.
Europe	United Kingdom	**PRS for Music** (Performing Right Society)	Collects performance (PRS) and mechanicals (MCPS) under one umbrella brand.
Europe	Germany	**GEMA**	One of Europe's oldest and most influential collecting societies.
Europe	France	**SACEM** (Société des auteurs, compositeurs et éditeurs de musique)	Historic CMO founded in 1851; major hub for French and international repertoire.
Europe	Sweden	**STIM**	Sweden's main performing rights society for songwriters and publishers.
Europe	Spain	**SGAE**	Sociedad General de Autores y Editores; national CMO for Spain.
Europe	Netherlands	**BUMA**	Often referenced alongside Stemra; commonly handles performance and mechanical administration.

Asia & Oceania	Australia/NZ	**APRA AMCOS** (Australasian Performing Right Association)	One network managing performance (APRA) and mechanicals (AMCOS).
Asia & Oceania	Japan	**JASRAC** (Japanese Society for Rights of Authors, Composers and Publishers)	Major CMO in one of the world's largest music markets.
Asia & Oceania	South Korea	**KOMCA** (Korea Music Copyright Association)	Primary organization supporting songwriters and publishers in Korea.
Asia & Oceania	Hong Kong	**CASH** (Composers and Authors Society of Hong Kong)	Hong Kong's key CMO for composers and authors; supports regional licensing and collections.
Latin America	Argentina	**SADAIC**	Sociedad Argentina de Autores y Compositores de Música; primary society for Argentina.
Latin America	Mexico	**SACM**	Sociedad de Autores y Compositores de México; key society for Mexican writers and composers.

Latin America	Brazil	**ECAD** (Escritório Central de Arrecadação e Distribuição)	Central office coordinating collections and distribution across multiple Brazilian societies.
Africa	South Africa	**SAMRO** (Southern African Music Rights Organisation)	Major collecting body serving South Africa and parts of the region.
Africa	Ghana	**GHAMRO** (Ghana Music Rights Organization)	Ghana's national rights organization supporting registrations and royalty collections.

Key Takeaway for Independent Artists:

You only need to affiliate with **one PRO** (typically the one in your home country). That home PRO then does the heavy lifting through **Reciprocal Agreements** to register your songs and collect income from the organizations listed above when your music is used in their territories.

Working with a **publishing administrator** (like Songtrust or TuneCore Publishing) can help ensure your songs are properly registered with foreign societies, which can speed up collections and reduce the fees taken by unnecessary middle layers.

II. SOUNDEXCHANGE

The organizations you are asking about are typically called **Neighboring Rights Organizations** (NROs) or **Phonographic**

Performance Organizations (PPOs), and they collect royalties on the **Master Recording** side of copyright.

SoundExchange is the designated U.S. organization for collecting *digital* performance royalties (a specific neighboring right). However, many countries collect **full neighboring rights**, including money from digital services *and* terrestrial/AM/FM radio, public venues, TV broadcasts, and more.

Here are major international equivalents to SoundExchange:

🌍 Global Neighboring Rights Organizations (NROs/PPOs)

Country / Region	Organization Name	What They Collect For
United Kingdom	**PPL** (Phonographic Performance Limited)	Public performance, TV, radio, and digital uses of sound recordings (often in coordination with PRS).
Germany	**GVL** (Gesellschaft zur Verwertung von Leistungsschutzrechten)	Royalties for performing artists and producers connected to sound recordings.
Australia	**PPCA** (Phonographic Performance Company of Australia)	Royalties when recorded music is publicly played or broadcast across services and venues.
Canada	**Re:Sound** (or *ACTRA RACS*)	Neighboring rights for performers and sound recording owners

		(often described as master-related rights in Canada).
Netherlands	**SENA**	Collections for performers and producers for public performance and broadcast use.
France	**Adami / SPEDIDAM**	Adami supports featured performers; SPEDIDAM commonly supports non-featured performers.
Brazil	**ABRAMUS / ECAD** (via specialized societies)	Several societies exist, with administration often coordinated through a central system (ECAD).
Switzerland	**SWISSPERFORM**	Collective society for performers and producers for neighboring rights collections.
South Africa	**SAMPRA** (South African Music Performance Rights Association)	Royalties focused on performers and rights owners connected to recordings.

🔑 Key Differences and Connections

1. **Scope of Rights:**

   - **SoundExchange (U.S.):** Primarily limited to **digital-only** performances (Pandora, SiriusXM, and similar services).

   - **International NROs:** Collect from **digital, terrestrial radio (AM/FM), TV, and public venues** (bars, gyms, restaurants). This is one reason international neighboring rights income can be significantly larger than U.S. digital performance royalties.

2. **Collection Strategy:**

   o **For U.S. Artists:** A U.S.-based artist should **register directly with SoundExchange**. SoundExchange has **reciprocal agreements** with many international NROs (like PPL, GVL, SENA, and others). This allows SoundExchange to collect a large portion of your foreign neighboring rights income on your behalf.

   o **For Non-U.S. Artists:** You register with your local NRO, and that society uses reciprocal agreements to collect U.S. digital royalties through SoundExchange.

3. **The Performer/Owner Split:**
   Similar to SoundExchange, many NROs split income between the **Featured Performer(s)** (often 45%), the **Sound Recording Owner/Label** (often 50%), and **Non-Featured Performers** (often 5%). Exact percentages can vary slightly depending on the country.

The most important move for you as an independent musician who owns your masters and is the featured performer is to **register all ISRC-identified recordings with SoundExchange** to activate the collection process both in the U.S. and internationally.

III. COPYRIGHTS

This touches the core of being a global, professional artist. The good news is that international music copyright is governed by treaties, so you generally do not need to register in every country.

International protection rests heavily on two key principles established by the **Berne Convention**.

Below is a breakdown of how copyright works for an international artist and what steps you should take to protect your music worldwide:

🛡 The Foundation: The Berne Convention

The **Berne Convention for the Protection of Literary and Artistic Works** is the main treaty signed by 180+ countries (including the U.S., UK, EU nations, Canada, Japan, and many others). It establishes two core principles:

1. **National Treatment**

- **Meaning:** If you are a citizen of a Berne member country, your work receives the *same copyright protection* in every other member country as that country gives its own citizens.

- **The Result:** If you are a Canadian artist, your music is protected in France and Japan as if you were a French or Japanese citizen.

2. **Automatic Protection**

- **Meaning:** Copyright protection attaches **automatically** from the moment the work is "fixed" in a tangible form (written down or recorded).

- **The Result:** You **do not** have to register in every member country to be protected.

⚠ **The Key Exception: The United States**

While the U.S. is a Berne signatory, it keeps a critical procedural rule for enforcement:

- **To bring an infringement lawsuit in a U.S. Federal Court, you must first register your copyright with the U.S. Copyright Office (USCO).**

3 Steps for Global Copyright Protection

Given the global environment, here is the strongest practical approach for an international artist:

Step 1: Formalize Your Ownership (The Non-Negotiable)

- **Fixation and Documentation:** Make sure your music is fixed (recorded/written) and that you maintain a clear, dated record of creation.

- **Split Sheets:** Create and sign **split sheets** immediately with collaborators (co-writers, producers), defining exact percentage ownership of the **Composition** and the **Master Recording**. This prevents ownership conflicts that can freeze royalty payments worldwide.

Step 2: Register with Your Home PRO and Publishing Administrator

Registration is not required for protection, but it is essential for **payment and enforcement**.

- **Register with Your Local PRO/CMO:** Register the composition with your local PRO/CMO (SOCAN, PRS, GEMA, and so on). This assigns an **ISWC** (International Standard Musical Work Code), which is crucial for tracking.

- **Global Publishing Administration:** The most efficient way to register worldwide is via a Publishing Administrator (**Songtrust, TuneCore Publishing, Sentric**). They register your song with foreign societies and help track and collect royalties owed under Berne-based systems.

Step 3: File a Formal Copyright Registration (Highly Recommended)

Automatic rights exist, but formal registration strengthens enforcement.

- **Register with Your Home Country's Copyright Office:** When available, this creates an official public ownership record.

- **Register with the U.S. Copyright Office (USCO):** Even if you are not a U.S. citizen, if you want the ability to enforce your rights in the U.S. market or against a U.S. company, **you must register with the USCO.** This is one of the strongest international enforcement tools available to you.

⚖️ A Note on Moral Rights

Many countries (especially in Europe) recognize **Moral Rights** more strongly than the U.S.

- **Moral Rights** include the right to be identified as the author and the right to object to "mutilation, distortion, or other modification" that harms your reputation, even if you sold economic rights. This is another reason strong documentation and clear agreements matter when licensing abroad.

IV. Music Reports (Music Licensing)

This is a major and valuable question. For an international independent artist, "licensing" in your home country (and beyond) happens through different lanes depending on the **usage type** (streaming, radio, sync) and the **royalty type** (composition or master).

The process is built on two concepts: **Collective Licensing** and **Direct Licensing**.

1. 🤝 **Collective Licensing (The Automated Royalties)**

    This system ensures you get paid when your music is streamed, broadcast, or played publicly. In your home territory, you license these rights through your national **Collective Management Organizations (CMOs)**.

The Right Being Licensed	What It Is	How You License/Collect
Public Performance (Composition)	When your song is played on radio, TV, live in a venue, or streamed (including non-interactive formats such as internet radio).	**Affiliate with your local PRO/CMO** (PRS, SOCAN, GEMA, etc.). By joining, you authorize them to collectively license and collect performance royalties domestically and internationally.

Mechanical (Composition)	When your song is **reproduced** (copied) onto a CD, downloaded, or streamed (interactive platforms like Spotify/Apple Music).	**Affiliate with your local mechanical society or mechanical division** (MCPS in the UK or your local CMO's mechanical wing) to support blanket licensing and collections.
Neighboring Rights (Master Recording)	When your specific recording is broadcast on TV, radio, or played publicly in venues (bars, shops).	**Affiliate with your local NRO/PPO** (PPL, Re:Sound, etc.) to license recordings for public use and pay you as owner and performer.

Key takeaway: You license these rights *collectively* to your national society, and that society (through blanket licenses) licenses them to users (radio stations, gyms, platforms) in your country and, via reciprocal agreements, in other countries.

2. 📝 Direct Licensing (The Negotiated Fee)

This is for specific negotiated uses where you maintain control and agree on a fee directly.

The Right Being Licensed	What It Is	How You License/Collect
Sync License (Synchronization)	Permission for your music (both **Master Recording** and **Composition**) to be synchronized with visual media (film, TV, ads, games).	**Directly** or through a **Sync Agent/Library** (Songtradr, Musicbed). If you own both sides, you negotiate the **upfront sync fee** and terms (territory, duration, medium).

Exclusive Master License	Licensing your finished master recording for a specific purpose (exclusive compilation placement, exclusive territory use, and similar).	**Directly** with the third party, defining usage parameters, splits, and contract terms.

Key takeaway: These deals are **transactional** (one-off agreements). CMOs usually cannot approve these for you, so you negotiate them yourself or through an agent.

💡 Summary for the International Artist

To fully license your music in your home country and begin collecting, you run two parallel tracks:

1. **Affiliate** with your nation's key collection bodies (PRO/MRO/NRO) to automate royalty flow.

2. **Register** with a **Sync Agent/Library** and be prepared to negotiate **Direct Licenses** for specific placements.

V. DISTRIBUTION

Since you are aiming for international reach, you need distributors with strong partnerships across hundreds of DSPs worldwide, including region-focused services in Asia, Africa, and Latin America.

The global distribution landscape is led by a handful of major services, many of which support audio distribution and, in some cases, music video distribution.

🎧 Global Music (Audio) Distribution

These services move your audio files and metadata to 150+ platforms globally (Spotify, Apple Music, Deezer, Amazon, Tencent, and more).

1. **The Market Leaders (High Volume and Reach)**

   These distributors often have preferred relationships with major platforms, which can speed verification and simplify delivery.

Distributor	Model	Key Advantage
DistroKid	**Annual Fee (Flat Rate)**	Best for **high-volume** artists releasing often. Fast distribution, useful tools like royalty splits, and quick Spotify verification for a low annual price.
TuneCore	**Annual Fee (Per Release)**	Strong global reach with tier options and support. Helps artists keep 100% royalties and offers publishing and sync add-ons.
CD Baby	**One-Time Fee (Per Release)**	Ideal for artists who release less frequently or prefer no annual catalog fee. Includes sync add-ons and physical (CD/Vinyl) distribution options.

2. **The Free/Commission Model**

   Good for artists starting out or prioritizing a free entry point.

Distributor	Model	Key Advantage
Amuse	**Free Tier** (commission) and Paid Tiers	Budget-friendly start. Free tier offers distribution; commission applies unless you upgrade.
RouteNote	**Free Tier** (commission) and Premium Tier	Flexible growth path. Choose commission-based free access or pay to keep 100%.

3. **The Label Service Providers**

   More selective options that offer higher-touch support, similar to a digital-label approach.

   - **AWAL (Artists Without A Label):** Selective; may offer advances and marketing help in exchange for commission.

   - **Symphonic Distribution:** Often used by established indie artists and labels; includes publishing, sync, and marketing services.

🎬 Video Distribution (The VEVO Channel)

Distributing music videos to channels like **VEVO** often requires specialized video distribution.

Video Distributor	What It Does	Key Platforms

DistroVid	DistroKid's music video distribution service.	Delivers to **Apple Music, VEVO, TIDAL, and Boomplay** (separate annual fee).
TuneCore	Video distribution available as an add-on.	Distributes to major video partners including **VEVO** and other channels.
Symphonic	Video distribution as part of broader services.	Delivers to **VEVO** and professional video networks.
Direct to YouTube	Your primary direct channel.	You manage uploads; your audio distributor can use **YouTube Content ID** to monetize usage (including your own official uploads if configured properly).

💡 Final Recommendation for Global Reach

For international artists, the most reliable route is usually a **Tier 1 distributor** (DistroKid, TuneCore, or CD Baby) due to global reach, solid analytics, and preferred partner relationships that help verification and availability across platforms.

Which of these distributors aligns best with your budget, the **flat annual fee** model (DistroKid/TuneCore) or the **one-time per release** model (CD Baby)?

VI. What should all international artist know about the music registration process?

This is one of the most important areas for international artists, because correct registration is what activates global royalty collection.

The foundation is understanding that your music carries **two separate copyrights**, and each has its own identifiers and registration path.

Here is what all international artists should understand about the registration process, organized by the two copyrights and their global tracking codes:

1. The Two Copyrights and Their Codes

A common mistake is thinking there is only one thing to register. You have two, and each uses different IDs.

Copyright	What it is	Global Tracking Code	Where You Get It
The Composition (The Song)	The underlying music (melody, harmony, lyrics). This is your **publishing** right.	**ISWC** (International Standard Musical Work Code)	Assigned by your **PRO/CMO** or your **Publishing Administrator** when the work is registered.

The Mas-ter Re-cording	The specific au-dio version you release and dis-tribute (sound recording).	ISRC (Inter-national Standard Re-cording Code)	Assigned by your **Digi-tal Distributor** when you upload/release the track.

⚠ **Critical Rule: Match the Metadata!**

Everything (**Title, Writer Names, Split Percentages**) must match on the ISRC side (Distributor) and the ISWC side (PRO/Publisher). If they do not align, platforms cannot connect the two copyrights, and royalties can sit unclaimed in a society's account.

2. The Three Collection Points (Where to Register)

You register similar metadata with three different organization types to activate revenue streams worldwide.

A. Digital Distributor (Master Royalties and ISRC)

- **Action:** Upload through a distributor such as DistroKid, TuneCore, or CD Baby.

- **What You Register:** The **Master Recording** (WAV/FLAC file) and release metadata.

- **What You Get:** The **ISRC** for the recording and the **UPC/EAN** for the product.

- **Royalties Activated:** Your **Master Royalties** paid through the distributor.

B. PRO/CMO or Publishing Administrator (Performance Royalties and ISWC)

-   **Action:** Affiliate with your national PRO/CMO, and for global coverage consider a Publishing Administrator.

-   **What You Register: Composition** data (titles, writers, splits).

-   **What You Get:** Your **IPI/CAE** number and the **ISWC** for the work.

-   **Royalties Activated:** Global **Performance Royalties** and global **Mechanical Royalties**.

C. Neighboring Rights Organization (Master Broadcast Royalties)

-   **Action:** Register with your national NRO/PPO or SoundExchange (if you have the international mandate).

-   **What You Register:** The **Master Recording** using the ISRC.

-   **What You Get:** Activation of global neighboring-rights collections.

-   **Royalties Activated:** Royalties paid to the **Master Owner and Performer** when recordings are played on non-interactive digital radio, terrestrial radio, and TV outside the U.S.

3. Common International Registration Mistakes to AVOID

- **Skipping U.S. Copyright Registration:** Even as an international artist, not registering with the **U.S. Copyright Office** means you cannot sue for infringement in U.S. Federal Court. This matters for enforcement.

- **Inaccurate Split Sheets:** Not locking ownership splits for the **Composition** before registration. If splits do not total **100%**, royalties can be frozen globally.

- **Inconsistent Stage Names:** Register compositions using the **exact legal name** linked to your PRO/IPI number. Mismatches are a major reason royalties get lost.

- **Registering Only Once:** Registering only with your PRO or only with your distributor is not enough. You must register **both the Master and the Composition**, and handle **Neighboring Rights** separately.

For any international artist, one of the smartest early moves is partnering with a **Global Publishing Administrator** to streamline the complex composition registration process across many countries.

Chapter 21: ORGANIZE EVERYTHING

In the complex world of music, where creative expression inter-sects with business operations, **organization is critical**. As an artist, your ability to properly manage music registrations and consistently track revenue streams often determines whether you get fully paid or quietly overlooked.

This section walks you through the **essential identification codes** required to register your music accurately, making sure you collect **every dollar owed to you** across performance, me-chanical, streaming, and sales income.

The Four Essential Codes for Music Registration

To function efficiently in the modern music industry, you must understand four core identification codes. Each one serves a specific role in identifying your work and protecting your ability to receive royalties.

Below is a clear breakdown of these essential codes.

1. ISRC (International Standard Recording Code)

The **ISRC** functions as your recording's digital fingerprint. It identifies a **specific sound recording**, meaning the finalized master audio file. This code is essential for monitoring usage across platforms and ensuring accurate performance and streaming royalty payments.

- **Where You Get It:** Assigned by your digital distributor (such as DistroKid or TuneCore), with **one unique ISRC per track**.

- **Who Needs It:** SoundExchange, Luminate/Nielsen, DSPs, and royalty tracking platforms use this code to identify recordings.

2. UPC (Universal Product Code)

The **UPC** identifies the **commercial product**, whether it is a single, EP, or full album. This code is required for sales reporting and inventory management.

- **Where You Get It:** Issued by your distributor, with **one UPC per release**.

- **Who Needs It:** Luminate/Nielsen, retailers, and chart-reporting services rely on this code for sales tracking.

3. ISWC (International Standard Musical Work Code)

The **ISWC** identifies the **musical composition**, which includes lyrics and melody. This code is fundamental for ensuring proper songwriter royalty distribution.

- **Where You Get It:** Assigned by your Performance Rights Organization (PRO) after the work is registered.

- **Who Needs It:** Publishing administrators, licensing agents, and SoundExchange (recommended, though optional).

4. IPI / CAE (Interested Parties Information / Composer, Author, Publisher)

The **IPI/CAE number** identifies **you** as an individual or entity within the global music rights ecosystem. It verifies identity across international databases.

- **Where You Get It:** Assigned by your PRO to your writer and publisher accounts.

- **Who Needs It:** All international rights organizations and music databases use this number for verification.

How These Codes Connect to Your Music Assets

Understanding how these identifiers relate to your assets is essential for staying organized:

- **Composition (Song/Lyrics):** Registered with your PRO, generating your ISWC and IPI/CAE.

- **Sound Recording (Master):** Registered with your distributor and SoundExchange, identified by the ISRC.

- **Commercial Product:** Identified by the UPC.

To maintain alignment between your PRO, SoundExchange, distributor, and publishing administrator, all codes must be logged accurately on a **centralized metadata master sheet**.

METADATA TO COLLECT

Maintaining a comprehensive metadata checklist allows you to register songs globally without delays caused by mismatched or incomplete information.

This system is divided into three categories:

- **Administrative Metadata** (release-level)

- **Composition Metadata** (publishing)

- **Master Recording Metadata** (distribution)

📝 Master Music Metadata Checklist for International Artists

Store all of the following information in **one secure spreadsheet** for every track you release.

I. Administrative / Release Metadata (For Your Distributor)

Data Field	Requirement & Notes
Product Title	Final, exact title of the single or album

Release Date	Official global release date (YYYY-MM-DD)
UPC / EAN	Universal Product Code, assigned by distributor
Primary Genre	Selected from distributor's genre list
Secondary Genre	Optional subgenre
Territories	Typically "Worldwide"
Explicit/Clean	Must be flagged correctly
Artwork	Minimum **3000 x 3000 px**, JPG or PNG
Copyright Line (Sound)	Owner of the Master Recording (e.g., **(P) 2025 Your LLC**)
Copyright Line (Composition)	Owner of the Composition (e.g., **© 2025 Your Publishing**)

II. Composition Metadata (For Publishing & PROs)

Data Field	Requirement & Notes
Song Title (Exact)	Must match distributor title
ISWC	Assigned after PRO registration
All Songwriters	Full legal names only
IPI / CAE Numbers	Required for each songwriter
Split Percentages	Must total exactly **100%**
Publisher Names	Self-published or company
Copyright Year	Year song was finalized
PRO Affiliations	ASCAP, BMI, PRS, etc.

Lyrics	Full text of the song

III. Master Recording Metadata (For Distribution & Neighboring Rights)

Data Field	Requirement & Notes
Track ISRC	One unique code per track
Featured Artists	Listed correctly as "feat."
Producer(s)	Full legal names
Mixer / Engineer	Full legal names
Recording Duration	MM:SS format
Audio Format	16-bit / 44.1 kHz WAV or FLAC
Performer Roles	Required for neighboring rights claims

The **most common cause of international royalty freezes** is mismatched song titles, legal names, or ownership splits across systems.

Collaborating With Other Artists

First, go to your App Store or Play Store and download a spreadsheet application (Excel or similar).

Building Your Split Sheet

Creating a standardized **Split Sheet** ensures composition metadata is captured immediately when collaborating.

The Split Sheet is the **legal source of truth** used by publishing administrators and PROs to distribute royalties worldwide.

It applies **only to the composition**, not the master recording.

Songwriter Split Sheet Agreement Template

(Complete and sign immediately after finalizing the song)

I. Song Information

Field	Required Detail	Notes
Official Song Title	Must match distributor title	Example: "Neon Sunrise"
Date of Agreement	Finalized date	YYYY-MM-DD
Date of Completion	Song completion date	YYYY-MM-DD
Recording Artist	Releasing artist	Your Artist Name
Samples Used?	YES or NO	If yes, list source

II. Composition Split Breakdown (Must Equal 100%)

Contributor	% Share	Notes
Writer #1	%	Example: 50.00%
Writer #2	%	Example: 30.00%
Writer #3	%	Example: 20.00%
TOTAL	**100.00%**	Required

III. Contributor Details

Data Field	Writer #1	Writer #2	Writer #3
Full Legal Name	Required	Required	Required
Role	Lyrics, Music, etc.	Lyrics	Music
Mailing Address	Required	Required	Required
Email Address	Required	Required	Required
Phone Number	Optional	Optional	Optional
PRO / CMO	Required	Required	Required
IPI / CAE Number	Required	Required	Required
Publisher Name	Required	Required	Required
Publisher IPI	If applicable	If applicable	If applicable

IV. Agreement & Signatures

Agreement Statement	Signatures
Ownership acknowledgment statement	Writer signatures and dates
Witness Signature	Optional but recommended

💡 Execution Tips

1. **Do it immediately** after the session ends

2. **Digital signatures are acceptable**

3. **Distribute signed copies to all contributors**

Producer Agreement (Master Recording Ownership)

The **Producer Agreement** governs the **Master Recording**, not the composition.

Your goal as an independent artist is to **retain 100% ownership of the master** while compensating the producer fairly.

📄 Producer Agreement Checklist

I. Scope of Work

Clause	Description	Importance
Project Scope	Tracks covered	Defines deliverables
Services	Recording, mixing, programming	Prevents disputes
Delivery	Deadline & format	Protects release schedule

II. Compensation

Term	Industry Standard
Upfront Fee	Non-refundable advance
Recoupment	Clarify royalty recovery
Producer Points	2–5% of net master revenue
Payment Method	Letter of Direction

III. Ownership & Rights

Clause	Preferred Language	Importance
Master Owner-ship	Artist owns 100%	Critical
Work-for-Hire	Required clause	Prevents ownership claims
Publishing	Separate from produc-tion	Avoids disputes
Clearance	Producer warranty	Legal protection

IV. Credits & Miscellaneous

Clause	Description	Purpose
Credit Provision	Credit format	Recognition
Portfolio Use	Limited permission	Industry standard

Final Action: Always pursue a **Work-for-Hire agreement with royalty participation** and have contracts reviewed by an entertainment attorney.

Course Module Review: 10-Step Music Business Coordination Workflow

Before registering any accounts, create a **Metadata Master Sheet** to serve as your single source of truth.

Phase 1: Foundation

1. Establish analytics accounts (Pandora AMP, Chartmetric)

2. Collect vanity URLs

3. Finalize PRO writer and publisher status

4. Register with SoundExchange

5. Prepare banking documentation

Phase 2: Metadata & Registration

6. Register works with PRO and distributor

7. Coordinate all codes in SoundExchange

8. Submit data to Luminate/Nielsen

9. Activate publishing administration (optional)

Phase 3: Legal & Public Protection

10. Register copyrights post-publication

Chapter 22: Best Advice for Setting Up Your Music Business LLC

Choosing the Right Business Structure (LLC, Sole Proprietorship, etc.)

This is an excellent and extremely important question, especially for independent musicians transitioning from treating music as a passion project into operating it as a legitimate business. Selecting the proper legal structure directly affects your **personal liability**, **tax responsibilities**, and **professional standing** within the music industry.

Below is the clearest and most practical guidance for setting up your music business, focusing on the two most common options: **Sole Proprietorship** versus **Limited Liability Company (LLC)**.

Choosing Your Music Business Structure

At its core, this decision is about weighing **simplicity** against **legal protection and professionalism**.

1. Sole Proprietorship (The Automatic Default)

If you begin earning money from your music and take *no formal action* to establish a business entity, you are, by default, operating as a sole proprietor.

Pros (Advantages)	Cons (Disadvantages)
Easiest & Least Expensive: No formal registration with the state and no startup filing fees.	**NO Personal Liability Protection:** This is the biggest risk. If you are sued (copyright disputes, contract issues, or injuries at a live show), your **personal assets**—home, car, savings—are exposed.
Simple Tax Reporting: Business income and expenses are reported directly on your personal tax return (Schedule C).	**Lower Professional Credibility:** Often viewed as less established by labels, publishers, sync companies, and investors.
Pass-Through Taxation: Income is taxed once, at the personal level.	**Unlimited Personal Liability:** Legally, you and the business are the same entity.

Best For: Artists who are just starting out, earning minimal income, and treating music as a side hustle with very low legal or financial exposure.

2. Limited Liability Company (LLC) (The Strongly Recommended Option)

The LLC is the most widely used structure for independent musicians, producers, and small labels because it combines **corporate-level protection** with **simple tax treatment.**

Pros (Advantages)	Cons (Disadvantages)
Personal Asset Protection (Limited Liability): Your personal finances are legally separated from your business. If the LLC is sued, your personal wealth is generally protected.	**Startup Costs & Ongoing Paperwork:** Requires state filing fees and, in many states, annual reports or renewal fees.
Professional Legitimacy: Establishes credibility with banks, distributors, labels, sync licensors, and industry partners.	**Financial Discipline Required:** You must keep business and personal finances completely separate to maintain the liability shield.
Tax Flexibility: Defaults to pass-through taxation, but higher-earning LLCs can elect **S-Corporation** status to reduce self-employment taxes (with CPA guidance).	**U.S.-Based Structure:** LLCs are a U.S. entity and may be treated differently in international operations.

Best For: Any artist generating meaningful income, signing contracts, hiring session musicians, performing live, or engaging in licensing and brand deals.

Final Recommendation for Independent Musicians: Form the LLC

For most independent artists, forming a **Limited Liability Company (LLC)** is the smartest and safest decision.

Why the LLC is the preferred structure:

1. **Liability Protection:** Music involves contracts, copyrights, collaborators, and live performances where accidents can happen. An LLC helps shield you from devastating personal financial loss.

2. **Tax Versatility:** The default pass-through taxation is simple, and the option to elect S-Corp status becomes valuable once net profits exceed roughly **$60,000–$70,000**.

3. **Business Foundation:** An LLC allows you to obtain an **EIN** and open a dedicated **business bank account**, which is essential for clean accounting and legitimate tax deductions.

Next Steps to Set Up Your LLC

1. **Choose a Business Name:** Many artists use a structure like *"[Artist Name] LLC."*

2. **File with the State:** Submit your **Articles of Organization** to your state's Secretary of State.

3. **Obtain an EIN:** Apply for a free Employer Identification Number through the IRS website.

4. **Open a Business Bank Account:** Use your EIN and formation documents to open a checking account strictly for music income and expenses.

And of Course... TAX WRITE-OFFS

This is where a properly structured music business really starts working in your favor.

Operating as an official business (LLC or Sole Proprietorship filing Schedule C) allows you to deduct **"ordinary and necessary"** expenses related to earning your music income.

Top Tax Write-Offs for Independent Musicians

1. Recording & Production Costs

These expenses relate directly to creating your music.

- **Studio Time & Engineering Fees**

- **The HITS Act Deduction:** Deduct up to **$150,000** in qualified U.S.-based sound recording production costs in the year incurred.

- **Session Musicians:** Payments to hired performers (issue **Form 1099** for payments over $600).

- **Software & Subscriptions:** DAWs, plugins, sample libraries, and collaboration tools.

2. Gear, Equipment, and Depreciation

- **Instruments & Maintenance:** Guitars, keyboards, amps, repairs, accessories.

- **Recording Equipment:** Microphones, interfaces, monitors, computers.

- Section 179 / Bonus Depreciation: Allows full deduction in the year of purchase (subject to current limits).

3. Marketing & Promotion

- **Advertising:** Meta, TikTok, YouTube, Google ads.

- **Publicity & Promotion Services**

- **Web Hosting & Domains**

- **Distribution Fees:** DistroKid, TuneCore, etc.

- **Visual Content:** Photography, cover art, music videos.

4. Professional Services & Administration

- **Legal & Accounting Fees**

- **PRO & Industry Memberships**

- **Business & Instrument Insurance**

5. Travel and Live Performance

- **Mileage:** Use actual expenses or the **standard mileage rate** (e.g., 67¢ per mile for 2024).

- **Flights & Hotels**

- **Meals (50% deductible)**

- **Stage & Performance Costs:** Wardrobe (not suitable for everyday wear), props, crew.

6. Home Office / Home Studio Deduction

If used **regularly and exclusively**, you may deduct:

- Rent or mortgage interest

- Utilities

- Insurance

  Using either the **Simplified Method** or the **Regular Method**.

Critical Advice: Documentation Is Everything

The IRS requires deductions to be **ordinary and necessary**.

- **Keep Finances Separate**

- **Track Every Expense**

- **Save Receipts**

- **Use Accounting Software or Detailed Spreadsheets**

Checklist: Documents Needed to Open an LLC Business Bank Account

Opening a dedicated business bank account is non-negotiable for protecting your LLC's liability shield.

Business Bank Account Checklist (LLCs)

I. Business Formation Documents

- **Articles of Organization / Certificate of Formation**

- **LLC Operating Agreement** (strongly recommended)

- **Business Licenses or DBA Certificates (if applicable)**

II. Federal Tax ID

- **EIN Confirmation Letter** (SS-4 / 147C / CP 575)

  - *Even single-member LLCs should use an EIN for professionalism and identity protection.*

III. Personal Identification

- Government-issued photo ID

- Social Security Number

- Personal contact details

- Ownership information for partners holding **25% or more**

Pro Tip for the Bank Visit:

1. **Call Ahead** to confirm requirements.

2. **Bring an Initial Deposit** (usually $50–$100).

3. **Always Sign in the LLC Name:**
   "Your Name, Member of [Your LLC Name]"

Once this account is open, route **all music income and expenses** through it to lock in your professional foundation.

Question 1. Can you distribute the same album in two different distributions?

For digital distribution (Spotify, Apple Music, and other DSPs), **no, you should not distribute the exact same album through**

two different distributors at the same time.

Doing this creates serious conflicts, and every major distributor and platform strongly discourages it.

Here is a clear explanation of why this happens, and what you should do instead.

Why You Can't Use Two Distributors for the Same Release

1. **Duplicate Content and System Conflict:**

    - Streaming platforms would receive two identical versions of your album or single, each containing the same **ISRC** (International Standard Recording Code, which identifies each track) and the same **UPC** (Universal Product Code, which identifies the full product).

    - When a platform detects that duplication, it can trigger several major problems, including:

        - **Removal:** The platform may remove **both** versions to prevent confusion in royalty accounting and metadata.

        - **Metadata Problems:** Streams can split between the two versions, which can cause inaccurate reporting, lost momentum, incorrect play counts, and wrong royalty allocations.

- **Duplicate Artist Profiles:** You can end up with multiple artist profiles, which confuses listeners and disrupts your branding.

2. **Royalty Payment Conflict:**

   - The biggest issue is payment. If the same track is distributed twice, the platform cannot reliably determine which distributor should be paid for each stream. The stores want one official source for each unique release, not two competing claims.

3. **Distribution Rights and Exclusivity for That Product:**

   - Even when a distributor calls itself "non-exclusive," most agreements still require that **that specific product** (defined by its UPC and ISRC set) is distributed through them alone to the stores they service. Trying to double-distribute can violate those terms.

What You *Can* Do Instead

While you cannot double-distribute the same release, you can use more than one distributor for **different purposes**.

Scenario	What to Do	Example
Switching Distributors	You must **transfer** the release. Upload the album to the new distributor using the **original ISRC and UPC** plus the **exact same metadata** (title, artist name, track timing, version names, and spelling). Once the new version is live and correctly linked, take down the release from the original distributor.	Moving your entire catalog from TuneCore to DistroKid.
Using Different Products	You can use different distributors for entirely separate releases or products, even if some tracks overlap.	Distribute a new full-length **album** with Distributor A, but release a separate **instrumental EP** through Distributor B.
Physical vs. Digital	You can use one distributor for digital delivery and a separate service for physical formats (CD, vinyl).	Use DistroKid for digital streaming and use a manufacturing or fulfillment company for CD/vinyl sales.

Key Rule: One unique UPC/ISRC set = One distributor.

Question 2. Can you strip an ISRC from a beat?

An ISRC (International Standard Recording Code) is a piece of **metadata** that functions like a unique digital fingerprint for a specific sound recording.

The short answer is: Yes, you can remove it, but it depends on the file format and where the ISRC was stored.

Here is the technical breakdown:

1. ISRC as Metadata

Most of the time, the ISRC lives in the file's **metadata tag**, not in the audio waveform itself.

- **For MP3, FLAC, M4A, and similar formats:**
  The ISRC can be stored in the tag system (for example, ID3 tags in MP3s). You can use a metadata editor to view, edit, or delete the ISRC tag, which effectively "strips" it.

- **For WAV files using Broadcast Wave Format (BWF):**
  The ISRC can be stored in a BWF metadata chunk. In that case, you typically need professional mastering tools such as WaveLab or a specialized BWF editor to remove it properly.

- **For physical CD masters (DDP images):**
  ISRCs can be encoded in CD subcodes. Changing that requires a dedicated DDP editor or professional mastering software.

2. The Exception: Watermarking and Fingerprinting

It is important to understand that while an ISRC is normally **metadata**, some companies also use technologies that behave differently:

- **Audio Watermarking:**

  Watermarking writes an invisible, inaudible signal into the audio that may carry identifying details such as an ISRC or a distributor-specific ID. This is much harder to remove because it is embedded into the sound, and attempts to eliminate it can reduce audio quality.

- **Acoustic Fingerprinting (Shazam, YouTube Content ID):**

  Acoustic fingerprinting generates a unique mathematical signature based on the audio itself. This cannot be "stripped" because nothing is embedded into the file as a removable tag. The fingerprint is created by analyzing the sound. You would have to change the audio significantly and re-render the beat, which alters the content and is still not guaranteed to bypass matching.

Summary: Stripping an ISRC from a Beat

Scenario	ISRC Location	Difficulty to Remove	How it's done
Standard Digital File (MP3, WAV, FLAC)	Metadata tag (ID3 tag, BWF header/chunk)	**Easy**	Use free or professional audio metadata editor tools to delete the ISRC field.
Water-marked File	Embedded into the audio waveform	**Difficult**	Requires advanced processing and

			may degrade the audio quality.
Content ID / Shazam Match	Acoustic finger-print stored in a database	**Impossible**	The fingerprint is computed from the audio. You must re-render with major changes to reduce matching, and even then it is not guar-anteed.

In most real-world beat licensing situations, the ISRC is typically in the easy-to-remove metadata field. If a producer wants to monitor usage, they usually rely more on watermarking and content fingerprint matching than on a simple ISRC tag.

Question 3. What distributions offer Gracenotes?

There are several routes for getting your music data into the **Gracenote** database, which matters because it helps identify music in CD systems, software players, and many car infotainment systems.

The most reliable methods are:

1. Digital Music Distributors (Aggregators)

Many well-known distributors include Gracenote submission as part of their delivery services, especially since Gracenote is used across major entertainment ecosystems. Look for distributors that explicitly list Gracenote as a supported "partner" or metadata destination.

Examples that often include Gracenote submission as part of certain packages or delivery options include:

- **TuneCore**

- **CD Baby**

- **Symphonic Distribution**

- **LANDR**

- **MusicDiffusion**

- **LabelGrid**

When you distribute, your distributor generally takes the release metadata you provide (artist name, track titles, album title, and credits) and submits it to Gracenote on your behalf.

2. CD Manufacturing / Replication Companies

If you are producing physical CDs, the manufacturing or replication company often offers **Gracenote registration** as an add-on service. This is common because they work directly with the final disc master.

Companies like **Disc Makers** and other professional CD manufacturers often provide this service, and sometimes bundle it with **CD-Text** encoding (which is separate and written onto the disc itself).

3. Manually Through Apple iTunes / Music App

Even though this is not a distribution service, it is still one of the most accessible ways to submit CD metadata:

1. Insert the CD into a computer running **iTunes (Windows)** or the **Music app (Mac)**.

2. Manually enter the correct track and album information.

3. Use the software menu option (for example, **Advanced > Submit CD Track Names**) to send the disc fingerprint and metadata to Gracenote.

Important Note: Gracenote is a **metadata identification service**, not a streaming store. You do not earn money directly from Gracenote. However, being properly listed ensures your music is identified correctly across players, car systems, and metadata-driven music services, which improves professional presentation and accuracy.

Question 4. What's the best approach for collaborating with other big artists?

Working with a major artist requires a professional, strategic, and value-driven approach. It is not about asking for a favor. It is about presenting a real business opportunity with clear upside and minimal risk.

Below is the best approach, organized into clear phases.

Phase 1: Preparation and Value Proposition

Before you reach out, you need to be positioned correctly.

1. **Have a "Banger" Ready:**

   - The most important starting point is having a finished, high-quality, professional track or instrumental sketch that fits their sound. It should be mixed and mastered to a releasable level.

   - The quality must justify their time and protect their reputation.

2. **Know Your Worth (and Theirs):**

   - Know exactly what you bring: unique sound, strong niche audience, production value, a concept, or budget support.

   - Clarify your "Why Them?" Your pitch must explain why that specific artist fits the track, showing you understand their current style and recent releases.

3. **Secure a Budget:**

   - Be realistic. Big artists often charge feature fees ranging from thousands to tens of thousands of dollars or more.

   - In many cases, the smartest approach is to lead with professionalism by asking, "What are your rates for a feature?" or stating that you have a budget. This signals that you understand how the industry works.

Phase 2: The Professional Approach

How you contact them matters as much as what you send.

1. **Contact the Right Person:**

   - **Best route:** their management or official business email (often listed on a website or social profile).

   - **Strong secondary route:** mutual connections. An introduction from a trusted producer, engineer, writer, or label contact is the strongest path.

2. **Write a Short, Professional Email:**

   - **Subject line:** clear and direct (example: "Collaboration Opportunity: [Your Artist Name] – Track for [Their Artist Name]").

   - **Message content:** keep it respectful, tight, and business-focused:

     - who you are and your strongest credential

     - what you want (feature on a single)

     - the value proposition and why it fits them

     - a private streaming link (SoundCloud private link, Dropbox link, etc.)

- the next step: request their rate and process

- Avoid attaching MP3 files.

Phase 3: Relationship Building

If cold outreach is not working, build an indirect path.

1. **Work in Their Circle:**
   Collaborate with producers, engineers, and mid-level artists who already work with them or their team. This builds familiarity through trusted channels.

2. **Network at Industry Events:**
   Conferences, showcases, and industry events create high-trust introductions and real-world visibility.

3. **Be a Real Supporter:**
   Engage online with genuine respect. Do not leave "collab?" comments. Show thoughtful appreciation. Make the pitch feel less random over time.

Golden Rule:

A collaboration with a major artist should be treated like a **professional business transaction** where you are minimizing their risk and maximizing their reward.

Question 5. What apps are best to help you write a hit song?

That is a strong goal. The most useful apps depend on what stage of songwriting you need help with: lyrics, melody, production, or collaboration.

Here are highly respected tools, organized by purpose:

All-in-One and DAWs (Digital Audio Workstations)

These help you build complete songs from idea to demo, including recording and production.

- **BandLab:** Free, cross-platform DAW for recording, beat creation, and collaboration.

- **GarageBand (iOS/Mac):** Free and beginner-friendly. Many successful songs begin as GarageBand demos.

- **Soundtrap (Spotify):** Cloud DAW designed for real-time collaboration.

- **FL Studio Mobile / Ableton Live / Logic Pro:** More advanced tools for professional production and arrangement.

Lyric Writing and Rhyme Tools

- **Songwriter's Pad / Lyric Notepad:** Lyric-focused apps with rhyming tools, syllable counts, and quick idea organization.

- **RhymeZone:** A popular rhyme and thesaurus tool used widely by writers.

- **Masterwriter:** A professional lyric-writing suite with deep phrase and rhyme resources.

Melody and Chord Progression Tools

- **Hookpad (Hooktheory):** Helps create chord progressions and melodies, with a database influenced by thousands of hit songs.

- **Suggester / ChordBot:** Apps that generate and recommend chord progressions in any key.

- **Ultimate Circle of Fifths:** A visual theory tool that helps with key changes and chord compatibility.

Collaboration and Organization

- **Songcraft:** Real-time collaboration for lyrics, chords, recordings, and structure.

- **Hum:** Captures and organizes audio ideas with notes about tempo and key.

- **Evernote / Google Docs / Apple Notes:** Still some of the most useful tools for lyrics, ideas, and quick drafts.

Question 6. How do I determine what points a producer is or deserves?

Determining producer points is a major business decision. **"Points"** refers to a percentage of the **master recording royalties**, and this is separate from publishing/songwriting royalties.

1. Understand What "Points" Means

Definition: Producer points are a percentage of revenue generated by the **master recording**. One point equals **1%**.

- **Major label context:** Producer points often come out of the artist's royalty share.

- **Independent context:** Points can mean a split of total revenue or net revenue (after costs), typically handled through distributor splits.

2. Standard Ranges

The range depends on the artist's status, producer demand, and budget.

Artist/Label Status	Producer Reputation	Typical Points Range
Major Label	Developing or newer producer	3% to 4%
Major Label	Established producer	4% to 7%
Independent / DIY	Standard benchmark	15% to 25% of net royalties

| Independent / DIY | Low or no upfront fee | Up to 50% of net royalties |

Note on net royalties: *In independent deals, "net" often means after production, marketing, and distribution costs are recouped, or it may be structured as a direct revenue split through the distributor.*

3. Key Factors That Change the Number

The final points are negotiated by balancing the **upfront fee** against the **backend share**.

Negotiation Factor	Impact on Points
Upfront fee / advance	Higher upfront payment usually means fewer points. A high enough fee can be a buyout with 0 points.
Producer reputation	A recognized or platinum producer can command more points.
Creative contribution	More creative leadership (arrangement, direction, sound) often justifies more points.
Risk level	If the producer takes no upfront fee and takes risk, higher points are justified, including 50/50 splits.
Included services	If they provide mixing and mastering, that can justify a higher share.

4. Separate "Points" from "Publishing"

Producer points are different from publishing. A producer can earn **points on the master** and also earn **publishing** if they contributed to the composition.

Royalty Stream	Producer Compensation	How it's Determined
Master Recording	**Points (example: 4% of master revenue)**	Based on contribution to the recording's sound and final production.
Publishing / Composition	**Songwriting share (example: 50% publishing)**	Based on contribution to melody, lyrics, or core composition. Beat-making that contributes melody often earns a share. Engineering only usually earns 0%.

Best Practice: Document the upfront fee and the points in a formal **Producer Agreement** before recording begins, so there are no disputes later.

Key Tips for Selling Your Lyrics:

-   **Build a Strong Portfolio:** Put together a strong collection of your best lyrics, ideally showing range across multiple styles, themes, and emotional tones. If possible, create simple audio demos too (even spoken-word over a beat or a basic melody) so people can hear how your lyrics translate in real time.

- **Understand Copyright:** Your lyrics are protected by copyright as soon as they are created in a fixed form (written or saved). However, officially registering your work with the U.S. Copyright Office (copyright.gov) provides stronger legal protection and enforcement options.

- **Define Your Terms:** Be specific about what rights you are selling or licensing (for example, non-exclusive use, exclusive use, or full copyright transfer). Always put the deal in writing with a clear agreement.

- **Networking Is Crucial:** Attend workshops, open mic nights, writing circles, and industry events to connect with collaborators and decision-makers.

- **Professionalism:** Be respectful, reliable, and timely, and deliver high-quality work consistently. Choose platforms that match your comfort level and your career goals. Starting with lyric marketplaces or freelance sites can help you get early momentum, but building your own presence and growing your network will matter most for long-term success.

Question 7. Can I have a BMI and ASCAP account?

No. As a **songwriter**, you can only be affiliated with **one performing rights organization (PRO)** in the United States at a time. That means you must choose between BMI, ASCAP, SESAC (or GMR, which is invitation-only).

Here is why, and what you *can* do instead:

Why you cannot have both as a songwriter:

- **Exclusivity:** PROs operate on an exclusive basis for songwriters. When you join one, you grant that organization the exclusive right to license the public performance of your works and collect performance royalties for you within their territory (the U.S.). If you were affiliated with two, it would create confusion over who collects what and could lead to double-billing issues for licensees.

- **Preventing Double Payments:** The system is designed so venues and broadcasters do not have to pay multiple organizations for the same performance rights coverage. If a song has multiple writers, each writer can be signed up with *different* PROs, and each PRO collects that writer's share.

What you *can* do:

1. **Choose One PRO as a Songwriter:** Select BMI, ASCAP, or SESAC (if invited). The decision often comes down to your personal preference, the type of music you create, and which organization you feel supports you best. Both BMI and ASCAP are strong and well-established.

   - **BMI:** Free to join as a writer, non-profit.

- **ASCAP:** Free to join as a writer, member-owned, non-profit.

- **SESAC:** Invitation-only, for-profit.

2. **Have a Publisher Account with Multiple PROs (If Applicable):**

   - If you also act as your own **publisher** (which is recommended, even if it is simply creating a publishing entity for yourself), you *can* set up publishing company affiliations with **both** ASCAP and BMI.

   - **Why?** Publishers may represent writers who are affiliated with different PROs. For example, if you are with ASCAP and you collaborate with a BMI writer, your publishing company may need a BMI publishing affiliation (under a *different* publishing entity name) to collect the publisher share connected to that BMI writer's portion, or to properly collect the publisher share for works you publish under that PRO relationship.

   - **Important Note:** Your publishing entity name must be *different* with each PRO (example: "My Songs ASCAP" and "My Tunes BMI").

Switching between PROs:

You can switch from one PRO to another (for example, BMI to ASCAP or ASCAP to BMI), but there is a formal process:

1. **Review your current PRO agreement:** Check membership length, notice windows, and any resignation requirements.

2. **Submit a resignation letter:** Notify your current PRO in writing within the required timeframe.

3. **Wait for confirmation:** This may take several weeks or even months.

4. **Apply to the new PRO:** Once your previous affiliation is officially ended, you can enroll with the new PRO.

5. **Register your works:** Ensure all compositions are properly registered under your new PRO account.

6. **Notify collaborators and publishers:** Let anyone connected to your catalog know the affiliation changed.

In summary: **As a songwriter, choose one PRO.** As a publisher, you *can* affiliate with multiple PROs, but you must do it under different publishing entity names.

Question 8. What are the best sites to generate music licensing deals?

When searching for the "best" sites to generate music licensing deals, it helps to understand that platforms fall into different categories. Each category supports a different path to licensing income.

I. Sync Licensing Companies and Libraries (Primary for licensing deals)

These platforms connect your music to film, TV, commercials, video games, podcasts, and other media opportunities. Many are curated, meaning they want professional, production-ready music.

A. Top-Tier and Curated Libraries (Often require submission and approval):

1. **Musicbed:** Known for a curated catalog and high-end placements with major brands and productions.

2. **Artlist:** Subscription model popular with creators; strong for indie artists and expanding into broader media assets.

3. **Epidemic Sound:** Major subscription service; often pays upfront for accepted tracks and may include additional revenue share structures.

4. **Soundstripe:** Subscription-based library with strong usability, also offering sound effects and video tools.

5. **Music Vine:** Curated catalog focused on professional film and video creators with strong filtering and licensing options.

6. **Marmoset:** Known for distinctive indie music with strong emotional and stylistic curation.

7. **PremiumBeat (Shutterstock):** Established licensing platform with high-quality tracks and flexible purchasing models.

8. **Pond5:** Large marketplace known for footage and also music licensing, often offering competitive royalty structures for exclusives.

9. **AudioJungle (Envato):** Huge genre variety; marketplace model with single-track buying and subscription options.

B. Hybrid and Specialized Options:

- **Music Gateway:** Sync representation plus services like A&R feedback and promotional support.

- **Lickd:** Unique model allowing creators to license recognizable mainstream music for YouTube use.

- **Crucial Music:** Respected placement company with strong film, TV, and advertising activity.

- **JinglePunks:** Broad licensing reach for podcasts, brands, and production needs.

II. Beat Licensing Marketplaces (If you sell beats to other artists)

These are designed for leasing and selling instrumentals to vocal artists.

- **BeatStars:** Industry-leading beat marketplace with storefront tools, licensing templates, and a massive user base.

- **Airbit:** Popular alternative, similar to BeatStars, with leasing and exclusive selling tools.

- **SoundClick:** Long-running platform for uploading and selling beats.

III. Digital Distributors with Sync Opportunities

Some distributors offer sync pitching or licensing services as part of publishing administration or add-ons.

- **TuneCore Publishing Administration:** Can pitch eligible tracks for sync opportunities through their systems.

- **CD Baby Sync Licensing:** Offers sync licensing features as an add-on for distributed artists.

- **Ditto Music:** Provides distribution, publishing, and sync-related services.

How to Choose the Best Site for You:

1. **Your music's quality and style:** Curated libraries want broadcast-ready, professionally produced music.

2. **Exclusivity rules:** Some require exclusive licensing; others allow non-exclusive submissions.

3. **Revenue split:** Know what percentage you keep and what the platform takes.

4. **Submission process:** Open upload vs. selective review varies heavily by platform.

5. **Target market:** TV/film supervisors, indie films, YouTube creators, beat customers, or brand campaigns.

6. **Ease of use and transparency:** Clear reporting and user-friendly dashboards matter.

7. **Your goals:** Passive background placements vs. actively chasing major sync placements.

Recommendation:

Most independent artists should begin with a few **non-exclusive libraries** to gain traction and learn what performs. At the same time, build relationships with music supervisors, editors, and production teams when possible. For beat sales, **BeatStars** and **Airbit** remain strong industry standards.

Question 9. How do I upload beat and see the ISRC?

This is an important question because it highlights how ISRCs (International Standard Recording Codes) work differently depending on whether a beat is being released as its own track or used as part of a final song.

ISRC Embedding and Beats

ISRCs are connected to a specific sound recording at the time it is officially released.

- **If you are releasing your own beats as standalone instrumentals:**

    If you plan to distribute your instrumentals to Spotify, Apple Music, and other streaming platforms, then **yes, each beat will need an ISRC**. Your distributor (DistroKid, TuneCore, CD Baby, and others) typically assigns an ISRC during the upload and delivery process. That ISRC becomes tied to the track in the distributor's metadata and is often embedded as part of the release delivery workflow.

- **If you are selling beats to artists to create songs:**

    In most cases, you **do not need to embed an ISRC into the beat file** you sell. When the artist adds vocals and releases the final song, **they** obtain the ISRC for *their finished recording*. Your role as a producer is typically protected through publishing registration and agreements tied to the composition, not the ISRC for the artist's new master recording.

How to Check for an Embedded ISRC

Some software can display embedded metadata, but the process is not always simple.

1. **Professional Audio Tools:**

    - **DAWs and mastering software:** Some DAWs and dedicated mastering programs can view or write ISRC fields in WAV/BWF workflows (depending on format and export settings).

    - **Metadata editors:** Tools like **MP3Tag** (Windows) and **Kid3** (cross-platform) are commonly used to view and edit tags for MP3/FLAC and may show ISRC fields if present or stored in a recognizable tag area.

2. **Check through your distributor:**

    - Log in to your distributor dashboard. Most distributors list the ISRC for each released track in the release details.

    - If you cannot locate it, distributor support can provide the ISRC.

3. **Online ISRC finders (for released music only):**
   If the beat or song is publicly released, online ISRC lookup tools can often retrieve the code using the song title and artist name (or a Spotify link).

    - **ISRC Finder (isrcfinder.com)**

    - **Music Gateway ISRC Finder**
      These tools work for public releases, not for unreleased files sitting on your computer.

4. **Specialized ISRC verification services:**

    - Some paid services (such as **isrc.com**) can verify ISRC details if you submit a file.

What to Focus On as a Beat Producer

If your main activity is selling or leasing beats, your priorities should be:

- **Copyright and publishing protection for the composition:** Register your beats with a **PRO** like BMI or ASCAP to protect your composer and publisher share.

- **Clear licensing agreements:** Use contracts that define usage rights, royalty splits, and responsibilities between you and the artist.

ISRCs are most relevant at the final release stage of a **standalone instrumental** or the **finished song recording** that the public streams and purchases.

Question 10. What and when do I get paid from my streams?

Music Licensing:

First payout can take 2 to 3 months. Music Reports pays artists on the following dates:

- 4th Quarter: On or around February 15

- 1st Quarter: On or around May 15

- 2nd Quarter: On or around August 15

- 3rd Quarter: On or around November 15

Spotify:

Before your first payout, you must wait 30 days (onboarding period). After that waiting period ends, you are typically paid every calendar month, usually within the last two weeks of the month. Spotify pays roughly $0.04 per 10 streams. So, 1,000 streams would be around $4, and 100,000 streams would be around $400.

BMI:

Your first royalty payment can take 9 to 12 months. Royalties must be collected by partner societies before being sent to BMI for distribution, and timelines vary depending on the country of origin. BMI pays quarterly in February, May, August, and November. To receive payment in February, May, and November, royalties must total at least $250 from all sources. In August, the minimum is $25. For direct deposit, the minimum is $2 per quarter.

ASCAP:

ASCAP typically pays U.S. performance royalties about six to seven months after the end of each performance quarter. With Direct Deposit, ASCAP can distribute as little as $1 or more into your bank account when it is ready. In some cases, it is possible to begin earning royalties the month after joining ASCAP if your music is registered quickly and performances are tracked properly.

SoundExchange:

SoundExchange usually distributes royalties within 45 days of receiving them. They will not issue a payment until the account is complete, there are no holds, and the balance reaches the minimum threshold. If royalties are under $100, SoundExchange will hold them until they reach the minimum.

Songtrust:

After registering with Songtrust, it can take 9 to 12 months to receive your first royalty payment. This delay is due to the time required for global registration and the processing schedules of collection societies.

TuneCore:

It usually takes 9 to 12 months to receive the first royalty payment, and up to 18 months for foreign societies. Based on average streaming rates, 1,000 streams on TuneCore is typically worth around $3.

DistroKid:

Earnings and payments become available once DistroKid receives and processes reports from stores and streaming services. Those services generally deliver reports monthly, but royalties for a song may not appear in your DistroKid account until about 3 months after the streams happened. Based on current payout averages, 1,000 streams through DistroKid are typically worth around \$2 to \$4 depending on platform, genre, and listener location, with Spotify often closer to the lower end per 1,000 streams.

The delay can be frustrating, but it matters because payments move through multiple layers of verification to ensure artists are paid correctly and fully.

Question 11. Why do I need Songtrust as an artist?

As an artist, you need Songtrust (or a similar publishing administrator) primarily to **collect all the publishing royalties your songs generate worldwide**, including royalties you likely cannot collect efficiently on your own.

Here is why it is crucial:

1. The Complex World of Music Royalties (Beyond Your Distributor)

When your music is released, it earns multiple royalty types:

- **Master recording royalties:** Paid to the owner of the sound recording (often you, or your label). Your distributor collects these and pays you.

- **Publishing royalties:** Paid to the songwriter and publisher for the underlying composition (melody, lyrics, chords). This is where Songtrust becomes essential.

Publishing royalties can include:

- **Performance royalties:** Generated when your song is performed publicly (radio, TV, venues, concerts, streams, YouTube).

    - In the U.S., these are collected by **PROs** like BMI, ASCAP, or SESAC.

- **Mechanical royalties:** Generated when a song is reproduced (streams, downloads, physical manufacturing).

    - In the U.S., digital mechanicals are collected through the **MLC**. Internationally, mechanicals are collected through CMOs and mechanical rights organizations.

- **Synchronization royalties:** For use in film, TV, commercials, games.

- **Print royalties:** From sheet music.

- **Micro-sync royalties:** From UGC uses like YouTube content.

2. Why You Need a Publishing Administrator (Like Songtrust)

Even if you join a PRO as a songwriter, PROs generally do not handle the full publishing collection process globally. Here is what Songtrust helps with:

- **Collecting the publisher share of performance royalties:** Performance royalties have a writer share and a publisher share. If you do not have a publishing setup, publisher money can go unclaimed or "blackboxed." Songtrust acts in the publisher-administration role to collect that share.

- **Collecting mechanical royalties, especially international:** PROs do not collect mechanicals. Songtrust helps access international mechanical royalties through its network of societies worldwide.

- **Global reach:** Songtrust has relationships with over 60 collection societies and pay sources across more than 200 countries and territories. Without that network, you would need separate registrations and systems across many regions, which is often unrealistic for independent artists.

- **Reducing administrative burden:** Registering works, tracking global usage, and handling society schedules and formats is time-consuming and complex. Songtrust handles these workflows.

- **Recovering unclaimed royalties:** Royalties often remain uncollected because owners are not registered or properly identified. Songtrust's metadata management helps reduce this.

- **You retain ownership:** Songtrust is an administration service, not a traditional publishing deal. You keep ownership and control. Songtrust typically takes a commission (often 15%) on the royalties it collects.

- **Transparent tracking:** Songtrust provides a dashboard showing earnings sources and activity.

When is the right time to join Songtrust?

- **When your music is live on streaming platforms:** If your songs are on Spotify, Apple Music, YouTube, and more, they are already generating publishing royalties.

- **If you write your own songs:** Songwriters are entitled to publishing income.

- **If international plays matter:** Global collection is where Songtrust becomes especially valuable.

- **When you are ready to monetize your compositions seriously:** Leaving publishing money unclaimed is a common mistake.

In simple terms, Songtrust acts as your **publishing administrator**, helping you collect publishing royalties globally, so you can spend more time creating music and less time managing complex royalty systems.

Question 12. What are professional booking sites for music artist?

That is a very strong question. Professional booking platforms are essential for music artists who want to secure gigs consistently, expand into new markets, and manage the live-performance side of their career like a real business. These platforms connect artists directly with venues, promoters, event planners, and private clients.

Below are some of the top professional booking sites and systems for music artists:

I. Dedicated Music Booking Platforms

These platforms are built specifically for the music industry and are designed to simplify the process of finding, applying for, and booking shows.

1. **ShowSlinger:**

    - **Focus:** A complete, all-in-one platform for booking live music, DJs, comedians, and more.

    - **Artist Features:** Free artist profiles, the ability to apply for gigs, manage show details (tech requirements, contracts, riders), handle payments, and ticketing. Artists often report fast payouts after shows.

    - **Why it's professional:** It is designed to replace scattered tools (spreadsheets, calendars, email threads) with one integrated system that keeps artists and bookers organized.

2. **ReverbNation:**

   - **Focus:** A long-standing platform in the music community that offers a wide set of services, including gig booking tools for artists, bands, promoters, and more.

   - **Artist Features:** Includes a free gig-finder tool. Paid plans provide expanded features such as industry opportunities, EPK creation, website builders, and distribution options.

   - **Why it's professional:** Its history, credibility, and multi-tool ecosystem make it a common hub for artists seeking a more complete platform.

3. **Gigmor:**

   - **Focus:** Modern booking approach that connects artists with local and national gigs, touring opportunities, and private events.

   - **Artist Features:** Unlimited gig applications with a Pro Plan (paid). Emphasizes faster matching and simpler booking connections.

   - **Why it's professional:** It reduces friction in the application process and can connect you to multiple gig types through one system.

4. **Indie On The Move (IOTM):**

   - **Focus:** A well-known resource for independent artists building tours. It provides an extensive database of music venues and booking contacts.

   - **Artist Features:** Free and paid options. Tools for venue research, pitch improvement, and notifications for availability.

   - **Why it's professional:** It is built around touring and venue outreach, with real contacts that help artists plan and route shows.

5. **SonicBids:**

   - **Focus:** One of the more established gig-booking sites, known for a structured and streamlined gig submission system.

   - **Artist Features:** Create a profile and search for gigs using filters like role type, location, and keywords. Used by many festivals and venues.

   - **Why it's professional:** It has strong reputation value and a broad network that includes serious opportunities.

6. **gigmit:**

   - **Focus:** A data-supported booking tool designed to match artists with promoters, venues, and festivals.

   - **Artist Features:** Free basic membership for an Artist Page (EPK) and limited gig applications. PRO membership offers unlimited access, analytics, larger databases, and improved ranking for applications.

   - **Why it's professional:** It uses performance data and structured profiles to support informed booking decisions.

7. **LiveTrigger:**

   - **Focus:** A free social network built by musicians for the live-music ecosystem, connecting bands, venues, bookers, and musicians globally.

   - **Artist Features:** Strong search filters, a community rating system, and a smart inbox for message organization.

   - **Why it's professional:** It adds organization tools to a community environment, which supports communication and booking workflows.

II. General Entertainment and Event Booking Platforms

These are broader platforms for all entertainers and can be excellent for corporate events, weddings, private parties, and high-paying local bookings.

1. **GigSalad:**

   - **Focus:** Connects event planners with entertainers and event professionals, including musicians.

   - **Artist Features:** Build a free profile (PromoKit), receive leads, send quotes, and accept payments through a secure system. Includes a "Worry-Free Guarantee" for clients.

   - **Why it's professional:** It provides a full pipeline from inquiry to booking to payment, and it is widely used for private and corporate gigs.

2. **The Bash (formerly GigMasters):**

   - **Focus:** Similar to GigSalad, connecting entertainers to clients for events.

   - **Artist Features:** Create a profile, respond to leads, and manage bookings. Known for producing a large volume of leads, especially for cover bands, DJs, and event-based musicians.

- **Why it's professional:** It has long-standing visibility in the private events market and offers structured lead-handling tools.

3. **Thumbtack:**

   - **Focus:** A broader local-services marketplace that includes event musicians.

   - **Artist Features:** Build a profile, receive leads, and send quotes. You usually pay a fee to submit quotes.

   - **Why it's professional:** Although not music-only, it can be a legitimate option for finding paid local gigs, especially for private events.

III. Niche and House Concert Platforms

These platforms focus on intimate, listening-based performances and house-concert circuits.

1. **Sofar Sounds:**

   - **Focus:** Curated live music events in unique spaces such as living rooms, boutiques, rooftops, and alternative venues worldwide.

   - **Artist Features:** Apply through the site. Typically perform a 30-minute set with two other acts. Guaranteed pay (often starting around $100 per show, depending on city and ticket revenue).

- **Why it's professional:** It offers a curated audience experience and can help build deeper fan relationships, especially for original music.

2. **Side Door:**

   - **Focus:** Digital booking and ticketing for non-traditional venues and virtual performances across North America and Europe.

   - **Artist Features:** Free artist profiles, connect with hosts, and create shows designed to strengthen community ties.

   - **Why it's professional:** It supports direct artist-to-host booking structures and encourages intimate performance environments.

3. **HomeDitty / Concerts in Your Home:**

   - **Focus:** House concert networks that connect artists with hosts who provide their homes as venues.

   - **Artist Features:** Often requires an application and sometimes a membership fee to access host networks.

   - **Why it's professional:** It supports the house-concert circuit, which frequently offers better pay and more attentive audiences for original music.

Important Considerations for Using Booking Sites

- **Professional EPK (Electronic Press Kit):** Most booking platforms expect a strong EPK: high-quality photos, a tight bio, music links, performance clips, testimonials, and accurate contact info. Keep it polished and easy to access.

- **Be Specific About Your Niche:** Clearly identify your genre, vibe, and ideal gig types so you attract the right opportunities.

- **Reviews and Testimonials:** Collect positive reviews from venues and clients. Strong reviews are powerful for increasing booking volume.

- **Responsiveness:** Reply quickly and professionally to inquiries and leads.

- **Networking:** These platforms help a lot, but direct relationships with venues, promoters, and your local scene still matter greatly.

By using professional booking platforms and maintaining a strong online presence, artists can expand live performance opportunities and earn more consistently.

Question 13. Where do I upload my merchandise product UPC's as a music artist?

As a music artist, you typically do not "upload" merchandise UPCs into one single universal database, unless you are registering them through **GS1** (which is optional, but can be helpful). Instead, you enter your UPCs into the **sales platforms** where your merchandise is listed.

A UPC is simply the product identifier that connects your merchandise in the store's inventory system to that specific item.

Here are the main places where you will input or "upload" your merchandise UPCs:

1. Your E-commerce Platform (Most Important)

This is the primary place where UPCs are entered. This step ties the unique number to your product listing details (title, price, photos, description) and tracks inventory correctly.

- **Shopify, WooCommerce, Big Cartel, and similar platforms:** When creating a new product listing (example: "Black T-Shirt, Size Medium"), you enter the 12-digit UPC in a field labeled **Barcode**, **GTIN**, or **UPC/EAN**.

    o **Important:** Each variation needs its own UPC, meaning every size/color combination requires the correct matching code.

2. Physical Point-of-Sale (POS) System for Shows and Touring

If you sell merchandise at gigs using a POS system (Square, Shopify POS, and similar tools):

- The UPCs you enter into your e-commerce inventory are what the POS uses when the barcode is scanned.

- The UPC functions like a lookup key: scanner reads UPC → POS searches the code → the product appears (example: "Artist T-Shirt, Size L, $30").

3. Major Online Marketplaces (Amazon, eBay, Etsy)

If you sell merch through online marketplaces, you will enter the UPC during the product listing process:

- **Amazon:** Amazon heavily relies on UPCs/GTINs and may require that the brand name matches the company name tied to that UPC in the GS1 database. You enter the UPC/GTIN in the product identifier field when creating the listing.

- **Other marketplaces:** You place the UPC into the platform's "product code" or "GTIN" field during listing creation.

4. GS1 Data Hub (Optional, Recommended if You Purchased from GS1)

If you purchased UPCs directly through **GS1**, you usually receive access to a GS1 tool, often called a **Data Hub** or product allocation system.

- **What you do there:** Register product details for each UPC, including:

    o **The UPC Number**

    o **Company/Brand Name** (your artist name or merch company name)

    o **Product Description** (example: "Black cotton unisex T-shirt with album logo")

- **Why it matters:** It creates the official record linking the UPC to your business. Retailers can verify that the code belongs to your company, which reduces listing errors and supports brand legitimacy.

5. Luminate/SoundScan (Optional, for Chart Tracking)

Merchandise UPCs are mainly for merchandise. However, if you sell a bundle that includes a physical music product (CD/vinyl) and you want those sales to count for music charts:

- You would register the **music UPC** (different from your shirt UPC) with **Luminate** (formerly Nielsen Sound-Scan).

- **Note:** This typically applies to your album or single UPC, not the UPC for your hoodie or T-shirt. Your distributor often handles Luminate registration for your actual music releases.

Question 14. Can you strip an ISRC from a beat?

An ISRC (International Standard Recording Code) is mainly **metadata** that acts like a unique digital identifier for a specific sound recording.

The direct answer is: Yes, you can remove it, but it depends on the file format and how the ISRC was embedded.

Here is the detailed breakdown:

1. ISRC as Metadata

In most situations, the ISRC is stored inside the file's **metadata tag**, not inside the audio waveform itself.

- **For MP3, FLAC, M4A, and similar formats:** The ISRC may be stored in the file's tag (example: ID3 tags for MP3s). You can use audio metadata editor tools to view, edit, or delete the ISRC tag, which effectively strips it.

- **For professional WAV files (Broadcast Wave Format, BWF):** The ISRC may be stored in a BWF metadata chunk. You would likely need mastering software like WaveLab or a specialized BWF editor to remove it correctly.

- **For physical CD masters (DDP image):** The ISRC is encoded in the CD subcodes, so altering it requires DDP editing tools or professional mastering software.

2. The Exception: Audio Watermarking and Fingerprinting

While the ISRC is usually metadata, some companies use systems that behave differently:

- **Watermarking:** An inaudible signal can be embedded into the audio waveform and carry identifying details such as an ISRC or internal distributor ID. This is far harder to remove because it is part of the sound itself, and removing it can reduce audio quality.

- **Acoustic fingerprinting (Shazam, YouTube Content ID):** This creates a mathematical signature based on the audio. This is **impossible to strip** without significantly changing the beat's sound, because the fingerprint is derived from the audio content.

Summary for Stripping an ISRC from a Beat

Scenario	ISRC Location	Difficulty to Remove	How it's done
Standard Digital File (MP3, WAV, FLAC)	Metadata tag (ID3 tag, BWF header)	**Easy**	Use free or professional audio tag editor software to delete the ISRC field.

Watermarked File	Embedded into the audio waveform	**Difficult**	Requires advanced audio processing, and removal may reduce audio quality.
Content ID/Shazam Match	Acoustic fingerprint (database reference)	**Impossible**	The fingerprint is not stored in the file. It is computed from the audio, so you would need major re-rendering changes to reduce matching.

In most beat licensing situations, the ISRC would be present only in the metadata tag and is relatively easy to remove. If a producer is tracking usage, they are more likely relying on watermarking or fingerprint matching than on a basic ISRC field.

Question 15: Do I need MEDIABASE if I use Luminate's submit form?

That is a critical distinction because **sales and streaming tracking** and **radio airplay tracking** are separate systems, even though Luminate may reference multiple datasets.

For **radio airplay tracking**, you must work with **Mediabase**.

🎶 Direct Answer: You Need the Mediabase Form

You **do not need a paid subscriber account** with Mediabase just to submit your song for tracking. You simply need to use their **New Music Notification Form**.

- **Action:** Complete the **Mediabase New Music Notification Form** (link referenced later).

- **Purpose:** This form allows you to submit audio and key metadata (Artist, Title, ISRC) so the song can be **encoded**, which helps Mediabase track airplay when monitored stations play it.

Why You Do Not Need an Account

Most independent artists do not need a Mediabase subscription. Paid subscriptions are usually used by labels, managers, and radio professionals who need constant access to reports, charts, and deep analytics showing where songs are spinning.

Your goal is simply to get your music **into the tracking system**, and the form achieves that.

The Luminate Google Sheet

The "Luminate Google Sheet" is usually used to register your **ISRCs** (tracks) and **UPC/EANs** (albums) so your **sales and streaming** data can be tracked properly.

Tracking Type	Organization to Contact	What You Submit
Airplay (Radio)	**Mediabase**	New Music Notification Form (audio file + ISRC + metadata)
Sales and Streaming	**Luminate**	Registration forms (often Google Sheets) for your ISRC and UPC/EAN

In short: use the Mediabase form for radio tracking, and use Luminate registration (often Google Sheets) for sales and streaming codes.

Question 16: What are the current direct links for the Luminate and MEDIABASE registration forms?

That is a smart move. Correct registration is the foundation for accurate tracking, reporting, and chart eligibility.

Here are the direct links for each:

1. Mediabase (Radio Airplay Tracking)

This form is used to submit your song's metadata and audio so Mediabase can encode it for airplay tracking.

- **Mediabase New Music Notification Form:** https://www2.mediabase.com/mbapp/newmusicnotification

2. Luminate (Sales and Streaming Data / SoundScan)

Luminate uses separate forms to register UPC (album or single release) and ISRC (individual track).

- **Luminate Album/Title Registration (UPC/EAN):** https://docs.google.com/forms/d/e/1FAIpQLScbwxd7bkIAB-BLz8xf9dLVRGHD-uSLn1kAIeHLYR2IIo-HUXQ/viewform

- **Luminate Track/ISRC Registration:** https://docs.google.com/forms/d/e/1FAIpQLSdsJbFiD

M_w6twCkftP6his8fc-
KIT2g3lWFgrDYR5AqPkRcA/viewform

Note on Luminate Forms: When submitting to Luminate, be prepared with complete metadata plus your ISRC and UPC codes, which should be assigned before you register.

Question 17: How do you use a label owner beat? How do you contact them?

That is an advanced and extremely important question. Using a beat owned by a label adds complexity because you are working with a business entity that owns or administers a catalog, not just a single producer.

Here is how to handle it legally and professionally.

1. How to Legally Use the Beat

When a label owns the beat, you are dealing with **licensing**, and you must obtain two separate permissions:

A. Master Use License (Sound Recording Rights)

- **What it covers:** Permission to use the actual beat audio file (the specific WAV or MP3).

- **Who controls it:** The label owner (or whoever owns the master).

- **Action:** The label must approve this license, defining your upfront fee, master royalty split, and usage limits (streams, downloads, term length).

B. Synchronization / Mechanical License (Composition Rights)

- **What it covers:** Permission to use the underlying composition (melody, rhythm, chord structure).

- **Who controls it:** The producer as a songwriter and their publisher (which may be the label or a separate company).

- **Action:** You must agree on the **publishing split**, meaning the producer earns a percentage of songwriting and publishing royalties collected through PROs and the MLC.

The Critical Agreement

You need a written **Producer or Beat Licensing Agreement** signed by you and the label. It should clearly include:

- Type of license: Exclusive or Non-Exclusive

- Upfront fee (or advance)

- Master royalty split

- Publishing split (composition percentage retained by producer/publisher)

2. How to Contact the Label Owner

Because this is a licensing request, treat it like a business inquiry.

A. Find the Correct Department

Avoid general demo emails. You want the right business contact.

- **Target:** Business and Legal Affairs, Licensing Department, or Sync/Clearance team.

- **Smaller labels:** Look for the label manager or owner email listed publicly (website contact page, social bio, LinkedIn).

B. Write a Professional Email

Keep it direct, respectful, and deal-focused.

Email Component	Content Focus
Subject Line	URGENT Licensing Inquiry: Master/Publishing Clearance for [Producer Name] Beat, [Song Title]
Opening	Brief introduction with credibility (artist name, stream numbers, notable wins).
The Ask	Name the producer and the exact beat title or ID. Explain you recorded vocals and need exclusive or non-exclusive master use plus publishing clearance for commercial release.
Usage	State intended use clearly (example: global distribution as a single).
Attachment/Link	Share a private, password-protected link (private SoundCloud or Dropbox). Do not send the beat file.

Closing	Ask who handles the standard agreement terms and confirm you are ready to execute paperwork quickly.

C. Follow Up

If you do not get a response within 1 to 2 weeks, send one polite follow-up. Be consistent, but respect the process.

Pro-Tip: If the label is a major (Universal, Sony, Warner), they may route you to the producer's publishing company for composition clearance and to master licensing for the master use license. You may end up dealing with two separate entities.

Do you know if the label owner is independent or affiliated with a major group? That changes the fastest contact path.

Question 18: Can I just give % for mainstream artist and producers without asking permission?

This is a crucial business question, and the answer is a firm **NO. You cannot use a mainstream artist's or established producer's work by simply assigning them a percentage without their direct, written permission.**

Doing that is a clear form of **copyright infringement**, and it can create serious legal and financial consequences.

The Legal Problem: Exclusive Rights

Copyright law gives the creator and rights-holder **exclusive rights** over the work. To use their music legally, you need permission granted through a license. Saying "I'll give you 50%" is not permission. It is like taking a car from a dealership and mailing them a payment plan without signing any agreement.

You need permission for two separate copyrights:

Copyright	What You Used	Who Owns/Administers It	The Permission You Need
1. The Master Recording	The actual audio file of the beat you recorded over.	The record label or the producer (if independent).	Master Use License
2. The Composition	The underlying musical structure (melody, rhythm, chords).	The music publisher or the producer as a self-published writer.	Synchronization/Mechanical License

Offering a percentage only explains how you plan to pay. It does not replace the legal requirement to obtain written permission.

What Happens if You Release Without Permission

If you distribute a song using an uncleared beat, the rightsholder has several strong options:

1. **Takedown Notices:** They can file takedown requests using Content ID and other systems. Your song can be removed from Spotify, Apple Music, YouTube, and more.

2. **Redirected Royalties:** They can keep the song online and claim **100% of royalties**, including master and publishing revenue.

3. **Statutory Damages:** In the U.S., willful infringement can carry statutory damages up to **$150,000 per infringed work**, which is far beyond any royalty split.

4. **Distribution Ban:** Your distributor may ban your account if you accumulate repeated copyright strikes that are not resolved.

The Correct Path: Split Sheet + Licensing Agreement

Before you release anything commercially, you must:

1. **Secure the Master Use License:** Negotiate the upfront fee and master-side royalty split with the master owner (label or producer).

2. **Sign a Split Sheet or Co-Writing Agreement:** Agree on the publishing split with the producer or publisher. This is required for registering with the MLC and your PRO.

Always get signed, written permission before distribution. Splits are part of the deal, but they are not a substitute for clearance.

Question 19: How does a musician get paid?

That is the single most important question a musician can ask. Getting paid in music is complicated because every single use of a song (a stream, a radio spin, a sale, a film placement) can trigger multiple, separate revenue channels that flow to different organizations and stakeholders.

A musician can earn money from **dozens of possible sources,** but they generally fall into three main categories: **Royalties, Direct Income Streams (Non-Royalty), and Fees/Advances.**

1. The Royalty Streams (Passive Income)

Royalties are generated whenever your copyrighted work is used. They are divided into two major lanes: the **Master Side** (the sound recording) and the **Publishing Side** (the composition, meaning the song itself).

A. The Master Recording Royalties (Paid by your Distributor/Label)

This is the income generated by the specific audio file you recorded and released.

Royalty Type	Source	Who Collects	Who Gets Paid
Streaming Royalty	Interactive streams (Spotify, Apple Music, Tidal). *Note: This is the largest modern source of master income.*	Your **Distributor** (e.g., DistroKid, TuneCore) or **Record Label**	The **Recording Artist(s)** and **Label** (based on your contract split).
Digital Performance Royalty (Neighboring Rights)	Non-interactive digital broadcasts (Pandora, SiriusXM, web radio). *Only applies to*	**SoundExchange** (U.S.) and international societies (e.g., PPL).	The **Sound Recording Owner** (Label), **Fea-**

	the sound recording.		**tured Artist(s)**, and **Non-Featured Artists** (session musicians).
Physical/Download Sale	Sales of CDs, vinyl, or digital downloads (iTunes, Bandcamp).	Your **Distributor** or **Record Label**	The **Recording Artist** (based on sales units).

B. The Publishing Royalties (Paid by PROs/MLC/Publishers)

This is the income generated by the underlying song (melody, lyrics, rhythm). It is generally split 50% to the **Writer** and 50% to the **Publisher**.

Royalty Type	Source	Who Collects	Who Gets Paid
Performance Royalty	Public performance (radio play, TV broadcast, live venue performance, interactive streams).	**PROs** (ASCAP, BMI, SOCAN, etc.)	The **Songwriter** (Writer Share) and the **Publisher** (Publisher Share).
Mechanical Royalty	Reproduction of the song (CD manufacturing, downloads,	**The MLC** (U.S. digital) or other mechanical rights	The **Songwriter** (Writer Share)

	interactive streaming in the U.S.).	organizations (MROs).	and the **Publisher** (Publisher Share).

2. Non-Royalty Income Streams

These are direct payments and business revenues that often matter just as much, and frequently matter more than streaming royalties early in a career.

- **Live Performances / Touring:** Revenue from ticket sales, guarantees, and performance fees at venues, festivals, or private events.

- **Merchandise Sales:** Income from selling physical products (T-shirts, hoodies, vinyl, CDs) at shows and online (Bandcamp, Shopify).

- **Sync Licensing Fees:** A flat, upfront fee paid when you license your song for use in a film, TV show, commercial, or video game. This is often paid through a publisher or licensing agent.

- **Fan Funding & Subscriptions:** Income through platforms like **Patreon** or **Twitch**, where fans pay monthly for exclusive access.

- **Session Work / Freelance:** Money earned as a professional instrumentalist, vocalist, ghostwriter, or composer for hire.

- **Brand Partnerships / Endorsements:** Flat fees or on-going payments from promoting a product or brand aligned with your image.

3. Fees and Advances (Contractual Payments)

These payments are more common when you sign a deal with a label or a publisher:

- **Advances:** A lump sum paid upfront by a record label or publisher when you sign. This money is later **recouped**, meaning it is paid back from your royalty share before you receive additional royalties.

- **Producer Fees:** A flat payment to a producer for their work on a recording, often paid through the label's advance.

- **Grant Funding:** Direct, non-recoupable funding from arts councils, foundations, or similar programs.

To maximize earnings, you must register your music with **the correct collection societies** (PRO, MLC, SoundExchange) so that every stream, broadcast, and usage converts into payments across all categories.

Question 20: What is the step-by-step checklist of the first five registrations every independent musician needs to make to start collecting these royalties?

That is a crucial checklist to build. As an independent musician, you should register with at least five organizations and secure two major codes so you can collect the full range of royalty streams tied to both copyrights.

The Independent Musician's Essential Registration Checklist

These registrations cover the two core copyrights of music: the **Composition** (the song) and the **Master** (the recording).

1. Affiliate with a PRO (Performing Rights Organization)

Why You Need It	Action	Code Acquired
To collect performance royalties (generated by radio, TV, live shows, and streams).	Choose **one** U.S. PRO (ASCAP or BMI). Register as both a **Writer** and a **Publisher** (using your own publishing name, e.g., *[Your Name] Songs*).	**IPI/CAE Number** (your unique rightsholder ID).

2. Register with The MLC (Mechanical Licensing Collective)

Why You Need It	Action	Code Acquired
To collect U.S. digital mechanical royalties (generated by interactive streams like Spotify and Apple Music).	Create a **Member Account** and register all songs, claiming the **Publisher's Share**. Your PRO	Your IPI/CAE is connected to the U.S. mechanical database.

	does **not** collect this money.	

3. Register with SoundExchange

Why You Need It	Action	Code Acquired
To collect digital performance royalties (neighboring rights) from non-interactive services (Pandora, SiriusXM, web radio).	Register as both the **Featured Artist** and the **Sound Recording Owner** (label/you). This is master-side only, separate from your PRO.	No separate code, but you submit **ISRCs** to link recordings.

4. Choose a Digital Distributor

Why You Need It	Action	Code Acquired
To collect master royalties from streams and sales (Spotify, Apple Music, YouTube, downloads).	Sign up with a distributor (DistroKid, TuneCore, CD Baby) to deliver your music and manage payouts.	**ISRC** (recording ID) and **UPC** (release ID).

5. Register with the U.S. Copyright Office

Why You Need It	Action	Code Acquired

To establish legal proof of authorship (essential for statutory damages and litigation).	File a formal registration for your works. Copyright exists automatically, but registration is required before filing a federal lawsuit.	Registration Number (formal legal proof).

Key Codes Summary

- **IPI/CAE:** Your ID as a songwriter/publisher (from your PRO).

- **ISRC:** Your recording ID (from your distributor).

- **UPC:** Your release ID (from your distributor).

By completing these five steps, you cover the major domestic royalty types for both the song and the recording, so you are positioned to collect your full earning potential.

Question 21: My song is done what's the first thing I should do?

That is the best feeling. Once the creative work is finished, you shift into **business and infrastructure mode** immediately.

The very first, most critical move after your song is mixed and mastered is:

1. Finalize All Agreements and Splits

Before sending anything to a distributor or registering anything, you need the legal foundation finalized. **This prevents disputes and ensures correct payouts.**

Action: Get a Signed Split Sheet

- **Identify all contributors:** List every person who contributed to the **composition** (lyrics, melody, rhythm, chords) and everyone who contributed to the **master recording** (beat producer, co-writers, engineers who negotiated a share).

- **Confirm the splits:** Agree on each person's percentage of publishing ownership. The total must equal **100%**.

- **Sign the document:** Create and sign a formal **Split Sheet** (or co-writer agreement) with everyone involved.

Why this is #1: Without signed splits, you cannot accurately register the song with your PRO or The MLC. If the record grows, unsigned splits can lead to a royalty freeze.

2. Register the Composition (Publishing Side)

After splits are signed, lock in your publishing registration:

- **PRO registration (Performance):** Log into ASCAP or BMI and register the song. This links your **IPI/CAE** to the title and your agreed splits.

- **MLC registration (Mechanical):** Register the song with The MLC to claim U.S. digital mechanical royalties.

3. Choose a Distributor and Submit the Master

This step puts the track on Spotify, Apple Music, and other platforms:

- **Pick your distributor:** DistroKid, TuneCore, CD Baby, etc.

- **Upload the master:** Upload the final mastered file (usually WAV).

- **Set a release date:** Choose a date **at least 4 to 6 weeks** in the future.

- **Secure codes:** The distributor assigns your **ISRC** and **UPC**.

Why 4 to 6 weeks: You need time for code assignment, Spotify editorial pitching, and coordinated marketing (artwork, press release, teaser content).

In Summary: The First Three Priorities

Priority	What You Get	Who to Deal With
1. Agreements	Signed Split Sheet	Co-writers, producers, collaborators
2. Registration	IPI/CAE linked to song title	PRO (ASCAP/BMI) and The MLC

3. Distribution	ISRC and UPC	Your digital distributor

Since the foundation is everything, the **first physical step** is getting that Split Sheet signed.

Question 22: Are you ready to jump into the 4 to 6 week pre-release timeline?

That is perfect. Since the music is finalized, the next two logical steps are locking the legal framework (Split Sheet) and planning the rollout (pre-release timeline).

Here are the templates and steps for both:

1. Split Sheet Template

A split sheet is a non-negotiable legal document defining the ownership of the **composition** for royalty purposes.

Required Split Sheet Data

Section	Data Required	Purpose
Composition Title	Full, exact song title	Primary identifier for the work
Date Created	Date the agreement is made/signed	Establishes timing of agreement
Total Split	Must equal **100%**	Confirms full ownership evidence
Contributor Details	Legal name, IPI/CAE (if available), email, phone for every contributor	Links contributors to PRO/MLC records

Contribution	Role (lyrics, melody, beat composition, arrangement)	Supports basis for ownership share
Signatures	Dated signature of every contributor	Makes agreement enforceable

Example Split Calculation

Contributor	Role	% of Composition
You (Writer/Artist)	Lyrics and melody	50%
Producer (Co-Writer)	Beat and track composition	50%
TOTAL	Full composition ownership	100%

Action: Use a professional template structure, fill it out immediately, and secure signatures from all contributors.

2. 4 to 6 Week Pre-Release Timeline

Giving yourself 4 to 6 weeks is a common industry standard for pitching, setup, and press.

Phase 1: 4 to 6 Weeks Out (Setup and Infrastructure)

- Confirm the final master file and high-resolution artwork are ready.

- Submit to your distributor with a release date at least 4 weeks out.

- Confirm your **ISRC** and **UPC** once the distributor processes the release.

- Register the track with your PRO and The MLC using the split sheet and ISRC details.

Phase 2: 3 Weeks Out (Pitching and Marketing Assets)

- Pitch to Spotify editorial through Spotify for Artists.

- Create a pre-save or pre-add link.

- Build your short-form video content and static visuals for release.

Phase 3: 1 to 2 Weeks Out (Hype and Activation)

- Announce title, artwork, and date across social platforms.

- Push pre-save reminders with strong CTAs.

- Pitch to blogs and independent curators (SubmitHub or direct outreach).

Phase 4: Release Day (Execution)

- The track goes live at midnight.

- Post "OUT NOW" content with direct links.

- Respond to comments, repost stories, and engage heavily to boost momentum.

Question 23: Can SoundCloud license an AI voice for me? And can I register that song?

This is a very complex area right now because licensing and legal frameworks around AI voices are still evolving. The answer has two parts: what SoundCloud can do, and what collection societies (MLC and PROs) will accept.

1. Can SoundCloud License an AI Voice for Me?

No, SoundCloud itself generally will not license a mainstream artist's voice for you. However, SoundCloud has partnered with certain **third-party AI providers** that offer legitimate, licensed voice options.

Scenario	Answer	Key Point
Using an unauthorized clone (recognizable celebrity voice)	**No**	Uploading a clearly identifiable, unauthorized clone is likely to trigger takedowns or claims due to copyright and likeness issues.
Using a licensed, partner AI voice	**Yes, indirectly**	You purchase the commercial license from the AI provider, not from SoundCloud directly. Monetization depends on being able to prove rights and licensing.

Bottom Line: You must obtain the license from the rightful source of the voice, either the real artist's authorized team or an ethical AI provider that secured legal permissions.

2. Can I Register That Song with The MLC and PRO?

Yes, you can register the song, but there are critical limits on who can claim royalties.

MLC and PROs focus on the **composition** (human-created lyrics, melody, rhythm).

A. Registering the Composition

- If you wrote the lyrics and the core musical elements, **you register the composition** with your PRO and The MLC and claim your shares (minus any human co-writer splits).

- The AI voice model is not listed as a co-writer or publisher because the U.S. Copyright Office has consistently held that purely AI-generated content is not eligible for copyright protection.

B. Master Recording Royalties (ISRC Side)

This depends on the AI platform's licensing terms:

- If you used an AI voice under a valid **commercial license**, the AI provider typically grants you distribution and monetization rights for the master recording you created.

- If you used a free or personal-only license, monetization is typically not allowed.

Summary for Registration:

Entity	Role of AI Voice	What You Register
MLC / PRO	Not a legal author	Register the composition based on human-created elements (lyrics, melody, arrangement choices) and claim your eligible shares
Distributor	Licensed element	Upload and collect master royalties only if your AI voice license allows commercial distribution

For safety and compliance, use ethical AI partners with clear commercial licensing, and avoid showing recognizable artist clones without permission.

Question 24: What's the top 3 scams in the music business?

That is an extremely smart question for an independent musician. A lot of scams target artists by exploiting ambition, urgency, and lack of industry clarity.

Most scams share one theme: **making the artist pay upfront for something legitimate professionals are normally paid to do.**

1. Pay-For-Play Playlist and Streaming Scams

- **The Scam:** Someone promises major playlist placements or guaranteed streams for an upfront fee.

- **The Reality:** Often bot streams or click-farm activity, which violates DSP policies.

- **The Risk:** Platforms can remove the track, freeze royalties, or ban the profile.

- **The Rule:** Do not pay for guaranteed streams or playlist placements. Pitching is either done through official tools or through legitimate marketing services charging for labor, not "guaranteed results."

2. Upfront Fee A&R or Fake Management Scam

- **The Scam:** Someone claims major credentials, praises your music, and asks for upfront money to "shop" your demo, secure meetings, or place you on tours.

- **The Reality:** Real A&Rs are paid by labels to find talent. Real managers earn by taking a percentage (often 15 to 20%) of income you generate, not by charging upfront for introductions.

- **The Rule:** Be cautious of anyone demanding upfront payments for "access" or "discovery."

3. Pay-to-Play Performance Scam

- **The Scam:** You are offered an opening slot, but must buy tickets upfront or pay a fee to perform.

- **The Reality:** You can end up paying to perform for little benefit. Legitimate venues usually pay artists, even if it is a small guarantee or a split of door revenue.

- **The Rule:** In most cases, you should not pay to perform unless you are intentionally renting a space for your own self-funded event.

Key Mantra to Avoid Scams:

¬ In legitimate business, money flows *to* the talent, not *from* the talent. If an "opportunity" demands upfront payment and sounds too good, it usually is.

Your independent success depends on **data, registration, consistent releases, and audience-building**, not expensive shortcuts.

Question 25: What should independent artist music post repeatedly?

That is the heart of modern music marketing. The strongest independent artists use a **content pillar strategy**. You should not repeat the exact same post again and again, because that can annoy followers and weaken performance. Instead, you post repeatedly within core themes that support your identity and drive interaction.

Here are four essential content pillars independent artists should repeat weekly or monthly, with short-form video (Reels, TikTok, Shorts) as the main engine:

The 4 Pillars of Repeatable Artist Content

1. The Music Pillar (Hook and Tease)

Goal: Drive listeners to DSPs and make the music recognizable.

Content Type	Frequency	Why It Works
Hook teasers	Daily or every other day (during release cycle)	Highlights the 10 to 15 seconds that stop scrolling and build familiarity
Lyric storytelling	Weekly	Explains the story behind one key lyric and builds emotional connection
"Song in use"	Weekly	Shows the mood and lifestyle fit, making the track feel usable and relatable
Call to action (CTA)	Every 3 to 4 posts	A direct, non-aggressive ask that helps convert views into streams

2. The Process Pillar (Behind the Scenes)

Goal: Humanize the artist and show the work, turning casual viewers into real fans.

Content Type	Frequency	Why It Works
Studio snippets	Weekly	Shows the grind and the real creative environment, not only polished results
Instrumental deep dive	Bi-weekly	Highlights unique sounds, gear, layers, and artistic decisions
"Day in the life"	Monthly	Creates relatability through daily reality and work rhythm

3. The Personality Pillar (Relatability)

Goal: Build a personal brand so people follow the artist, not only the songs.

Content Type	Frequency	Why It Works
Influences and reactions	Weekly	Attracts fans of similar artists and shows taste and identity
Q&A and interactive	Bi-weekly	Builds connection through direct fan engagement and answers
Life and hobbies	Monthly	Adds depth and makes the artist feel real and multi-dimensional

4. The Live/Performance Pillar

Goal: Drive ticket sales and show the energy of the music in real environments.

Content Type	Frequency	Why It Works
Raw performance clips	Weekly	Captures authenticity and shows talent without heavy production
Concert teasers	As needed	Creates urgency and awareness for shows and local events
Fan shout-outs (UGC)	Weekly	Builds community and rewards audience participation

The Golden Rule for Repetition: The 80/20 Rule

To avoid sounding overly promotional:

- **80%** should be entertainment, education, process, or personality (pillars 2, 3, 4).

- **20%** should be direct promotion (pillar 1).

Consistency inside these pillars matters more than pure volume. Three strong posts per week can outperform daily low-effort promotions.

Chapter 23: GRAB A PENCIL, Quiz Time!

This Quiz is to Help You Review

This is a fantastic idea to test your knowledge of the music registration process!

Here is a **20-Question Quiz** covering the essentials of accounts, codes, and the "why" behind registering your music.

Music Registration & Royalties Quiz (20 Questions)

Part 1: The Essential Organizations (Q1–Q6)

Q1. (True/False): Your Distributor (e.g., DistroKid, TuneCore) is responsible for collecting your performance royalties.

A. True

B. False

Q2. Multiple Choice: Which organization is responsible for collecting the **Publisher's Share** of **Digital Mechanical Royalties** for streams in the United States?

A. ASCAP

B. BMI

C. The MLC

D. SoundExchange

Q3. Multiple Choice: Which type of organization primarily collects royalties for the **Public Performance** of your song (e.g., radio play, streaming, TV broadcast)?

A. A Publisher Administrator (like Songtrust)

B. A Sound Recording Collective (like PPL or SoundExchange)

C. A Performing Rights Organization (PRO)

D. The Copyright Office

Q4. (True/False): A songwriter can be affiliated with both ASCAP and BMI simultaneously as a writer.

A. True

B. False

Q5. Fill-in-the-Blank: The organization that collects **digital performance royalties** for the **sound recording** (the "master") from non-interactive streams like Pandora or SiriusXM is

_____.

Q6. Multiple Choice: If you are a Canadian writer, which organization handles your mechanical royalties for streams **within Canada**?

A. The MLC

B. BMI

C. CMRRA

D. RIAA

Part 2: The Essential Codes (Q7–Q12)

Q7. Multiple Choice: Which 12-character code uniquely identifies a specific **sound recording** (the master track), and is assigned by your distributor?

A. IPI

B. ISWC

C. ISRC

D. ISBN

Q8. Multiple Choice: Which unique code identifies you, the **songwriter or publisher**, as an interested party in the music industry?

A. ISRC

B. IPI / CAE Number

C. UPC

D. ASIN

Q9. (True/False): The ISRC for an acoustic version of a song will be the same as the ISRC for the studio version of that same song.

A. True

B. False

Q10. Multiple Choice: What is the 13-digit code used to identify a **book** (print or electronic format), which is often represented in a barcode?

A. ISRC

B. ISBN

C. UPC

D. IPI

Q11. Multiple Choice: Which code is primarily used by PROs to identify the **musical work** (the composition) globally?

A. ISRC

B. ISWC

C. UPC

D. ASIN

Q12. Fill-in-the-Blank: The code required to track radio airplay and feed data to Luminate charts is primarily handled by _____ data.

Part 3: Understanding Royalties and Splits (Q13–Q17)

Q13. Multiple Choice: Which royalty stream is generated when a song is streamed **on-demand** (i.e., you chose the song) on Spotify in the U.S.?

A. Performance Royalty only

B. Mechanical Royalty only

C. Both Performance and Mechanical Royalties

D. Neighboring Rights Royalty only

Q14. Multiple Choice: If a song is 50% Publisher Share and 50% Writer Share, and you are the sole writer, what share of the song should you claim when registering your **Writer** affiliation with your PRO?

A. 50%

B. 100%

C. 25%

D. 75%

Q15. (True/False): When registering a co-written song with a collective (PRO or MLC), the total splits submitted for all writers and publishers must always add up to 100%.

A. True

B. False

Q16. Multiple Choice: The term for the historical, unmatched mechanical royalties that The MLC is currently working to distribute is often called:

A. Black Box Royalties

B. Deferred Income

C. Unreconciled Funds

D. Residual Payouts

Q17. (True/False): When you join The MLC, your PRO will automatically stop collecting your performance royalties.

A. True

B. False

Part 4: Registration Process (Q18–Q20)

Q18. Multiple Choice: Which organization requires you to pay a fee to register and protect your intellectual property as a legal record in the United States?

A. ASCAP/BMI

B. The MLC

C. The U.S. Copyright Office

D. Mediabase

Q19. Multiple Choice: When registering a song with The MLC, which party is typically listed as the rightsholder for the **Publisher Share**?

A. Your Music Distributor

B. Your MLC Member Name (e.g., [Your Name] Songs)

C. The Recording Artist (if different from the writer)

D. The Record Label

Q20. Multiple Choice: What is the primary purpose of registering your music with **Mediabase**?

A. To collect synchronization fees from TV shows.

B. To ensure your radio airplay is tracked for chart reporting.

C. To receive physical CD sales reports.

D. To manage your international mechanical royalties.

Answer Key

Q#	Answer	Explanation
Q1	B. False	Distributors handle the master recording (sound recording) royalties, not the publishing (song composition) royalties.
Q2	C. The MLC	The MLC is the sole body collecting U.S. digital mechanical royalties from streaming services.
Q3	C. A Performing Rights Organization (PRO)	PROs (ASCAP, BMI, etc.) specialize in the public performance income.
Q4	B. False	A writer can only affiliate with one PRO at a time for U.S. performance rights.
Q5	SoundExchange	SoundExchange collects the *master* side of non-interactive digital performance royalties (Neighboring Rights).
Q6	C. CMRRA	CMRRA or SOCAN Reproduction Rights handle mechanicals for streams within Canada.
Q7	C. ISRC	The ISRC is the International Standard Recording Code.
Q8	B. IPI / CAE Number	The IPI (Interested Party Information) number identifies people and companies in the publishing world.

Q9	B. False	Each unique *recording* requires its own ISRC.
Q10	B. ISBN	ISBN (International Standard Book Number) is for books.
Q11	B. ISWC	The ISWC (International Standard Musical Work Code) is the identifier for the song composition itself.
Q12	Mediabase	Luminate uses Mediabase data to power its radio airplay charts.
Q13	C. Both Performance and Mechanical Royalties	Interactive streams generate both types of publishing royalties.
Q14	B. 100%	The 50% is your *share of the writer side*. When you register, you register your 100% writer side ownership of the song.
Q15	A. True	All splits for a song must total 100% to ensure the song's ownership is fully claimed.
Q16	A. Black Box Royalties	This is the common industry term for the billions of unmatched royalties.
Q17	B. False	The MLC and your PRO handle entirely different types of royalties and operate independently.
Q18	C. The U.S. Copyright Office	Copyright registration is a one-time, paid legal process that is separate from royalty collection.

Q19	B. Your MLC Member Name	As a self-administered writer, your Member Name is the entity that claims the publisher's share.
Q20	B. To ensure your radio airplay is tracked for chart reporting.	Mediabase is a radio airplay monitoring service.

Conclusion: Your Journey Begins

- Reinforcement of the core message: Your music is your art, and your metadata is your paycheck.

- Call to action: Embrace your independence, master the business, and create fearlessly.

Chapter 24: Links to Registration Platforms and Tool

That's an essential list! Having the direct links to these platforms will save you significant time and ensure your music is registered correctly with the official entities.

Here are the official registration portals and tools based on the accounts, codes, and data we discussed:

🔗 Royalty Collection & Tracking Platforms

These links are for creating the accounts necessary to collect money and track performance/airplay data.

Organization	Purpose	Official Registration/Login Link
The MLC (Mechanical Licensing Collective)	Collects **U.S. Digital Mechanical Royalties** from streaming services (crucial for publishers and self-administered writers).	The MLC Portal: Sign Up
ASCAP (Performing Rights Organization)	Collects **Performance Royalties** (writer and publisher shares) in the U.S.	ASCAP Join Page
BMI (Performing Rights Organization)	Collects **Performance Royalties** (writer and publisher shares) in the U.S.	BMI Creators Page (Includes Join Link)

Mediabase	Tracks **Radio Airplay** (critical for charting, as the data is used by Luminate and Billboard).	Mediabase New Music Notification Form
U.S. Copyright Office	Registers the **legal copyright** (composition and/or sound recording) for protection.	eCO Registration System (Login/Start Claim)

Essential Codes & Identifiers

Remember that your **ISRC** (International Standard Recording Code) is assigned and provided to you by your **music distributor** (e.g., DistroKid, TuneCore, CD Baby) upon distribution.

Your **IPI/CAE Number** is assigned to you **automatically** when you successfully affiliate as a writer with a PRO (ASCAP, BMI, etc.). You will find this number in your member portal after approval.

The End of Confusion. The Start of Control.**

The era of waiting for permission is over. You have learned that the path to a sustainable independent career is paved with **data integrity, accurate registration, and self-advocacy.**

The codes, ISRC, IPI, ISBN, are not roadblocks; they are the tools of your trade. The organizations, PROs, MLC, SoundExchange, are not gatekeepers; they are your partners in collection.

The independent music business is not a mystery; it is a system. And now, you run the system.

Thank you for taking this journey. Now, close this book, log into your Accounts, and get to work. Your royalties are waiting!